J
É
S
U
S

ROSE
FOR
YOU

JESUS

ROSE
FOR
YOU

CHARLES SPURGEON

Whitaker House

All Scripture quotations are taken from the *King James Version* (KJV) of the Bible.

JESUS ROSE FOR YOU

ISBN: 0-88368-507-8
Printed in the United States of America
Copyright © 1998 by Whitaker House

Whitaker House
30 Hunt Valley Circle
New Kensington, PA 15068

Library of Congress Cataloging-in-Publication Data

Spurgeon, C. H. (Charles Haddon), 1834–1892
    Jesus rose for you / by Charles Spurgeon.
        p.   cm.
    ISBN 0-88368-507-8
    1. Jesus Christ—Resurrection. 2. Resurrection. I. Title.
  BT481.S73 1998
  232'.5—dc21   98-12617

1 2 3 4 5 6 7 8 9 10 11 12 / 08 07 06 05 04 03 02 01 00 99 98

CONTENTS

1. The Stone Rolled Away 7

2. A Visit to the Tomb 27

3. Christ, the Destroyer of Death............................ 45

4. Great Truths of the Resurrection....................... 65

5. All Power in Heaven and Earth.......................... 83

6. Being Resurrected with Christ 105

7. Following the Risen Lord 125

8. Will There Be a Future Bodily Resurrection?...147

9. The Power of Christ Revealed 169

10. The Coming Resurrection 187

Chapter One

The Stone Rolled Away

*The angel of the Lord descended from heaven, and came
and rolled back the stone from the door, and sat upon it.*
—Matthew 28:2

The Lord Jesus Christ was crucified just hours before the Sabbath day began. According to Jewish law, His body had to buried before the Sabbath. Therefore, Joseph of Arimathea, a wealthy Pharisee who believed in Jesus, wrapped His body in fine linen, placed it in a new tomb, and rolled a heavy stone against the entrance. Mary Magdalene and other women who had followed Jesus during His ministry, and who had mourned His crucifixion, saw where Joseph placed Jesus' body.

At dawn on the first day of the week after the Sabbath, Mary Magdalene and another woman named Mary went toward the sepulcher. They wanted to embalm the body of Jesus, but they remembered that the huge stone at the door of the tomb would be a great obstacle in their way. They said to one another, *"Who shall roll us away the stone?"* (Mark 16:3).

That simple question encompasses the mournful inquiry of the entire universe. The women seem to have put into language the great sigh of universal mankind:

"Who shall roll us away the stone?" In man's path of happiness lay a huge rock that completely blocked the road: the inevitability of death. Who among the mighty could remove the barrier? Philosophy attempted the task but failed miserably. In man's age-old quest for immortality, the stone of doubt, uncertainty, and unbelief stopped all progress. Who could lift the formidable mass of death and destruction and bring life and immortality to light (2 Timothy 1:10)?

For generation after generation, men have buried their fellowmen; the all-devouring sepulcher has swallowed its multitudes. From ancient times, people have asked, "Who can stop the daily slaughter or give hope for life beyond the grave?" Yes, there was a whisper of a resurrection, but men could not believe in it. Some dreamed of a future state and talked of it in mysterious poetry, as though it were all imagination and nothing more. In darkness and in twilight, with many fears and few guesses at the truth, men inquired, *"Who shall roll us away the stone?"*

For the women who visited Jesus' tomb, there were three difficulties: the stone itself was huge; it was stamped with the seal of Roman law; and it was guarded by the representatives of power. For mankind, there were the same three difficulties. Death itself was a huge stone, not to be moved by any strength known to mortals. Death was clearly sent by God as a penalty for offenses against His law. Therefore, how could it be averted; how could it be removed? The red seal of God's vengeance was affixed on that sepulcher's mouth—how could that seal be broken? Who could roll away the stone?

No answer was given to philosophers and kings, but the women who loved the Savior found an answer. They came to the tomb of Christ, but it was empty, for Jesus had risen. Here is the answer to the world's inquiry: there is another life. Bodies will live again, for Jesus lives. Do not grieve any longer around the grave, you mourners, as those who are without hope, for since Jesus Christ is risen, the dead in Christ will rise also. Wipe away those tears, for the believer's grave is no longer a place of mourning. It is now the passage to immortality.

I want to begin this book by presenting you with some of the major implications of the resurrection of our exalted Lord Jesus. To illustrate these truths, I will discuss what it means for us that the stone of Jesus' tomb was rolled away. Then I will invite you to hear the angel's message, which he gave from his position on top of the stone.

THE MESSAGE OF THE STONE

I call the stone as my first witness. It is not an uncommon thing at all to find incidences in the Scriptures where stones were commanded to be witnesses. Great stones were placed as witnesses against the people of Israel (Joshua 24:26–27; 1 Samuel 14:33), and a stone and beam out of the wall were called upon to testify to sin (Habakkuk 2:10–11). Therefore, I will call this stone of Jesus' tomb as a witness to valuable truths of which it was the symbol. The river of my thought divides into six streams.

The Door of the Sepulcher Removed

First, the stone that was rolled away must clearly be regarded as the door that was removed from the sepulcher of death. Death's house was firmly secured by a huge stone; however, the angel removed it, and the living Christ came forth. Notice that the massive door was taken away from the grave—not merely opened, but un-hinged, flung aside, rolled away—and from that time on, death's ancient prison has been without a door. Believers will still go into it, but they will not be shut in. They will stay there as in an open cave, but there is nothing to prevent them from coming out of it in due time.

In the Old Testament, we read how Samson was sur-rounded by his enemies at night when he stayed in Gaza (Judges 16:1–3). However, he arose at midnight and put the gates of the city on his shoulders—post, bar, and all. He carried everything away and left the Philistine stronghold open and exposed. Our Master did the same thing to the grave. Having slept out His three days and nights according to the divine decree (Matthew 12:39–40), He arose in the greatness of His strength and car-ried away the iron gates of the sepulcher, tearing every bar from its place. The removal of the stone from the sepulcher was an outward symbol that our Lord had pulled up the gates of the grave—post, bar, and all—thus exposing that old fortress of death and hell and leaving it as a city that has been stormed and taken, and is there-fore bereft of power.

Remember that our Lord was committed to the grave as a hostage: "[He] *was delivered for our offences*" (Romans 4:25). Our sins were charged to Him like a debt. On the cross, He discharged the debt of obligation that we owed God. Jesus was our great Substitute. He suf-fered to the fullest, in proportion to the punishment that we deserved. After this, He was confined in the tomb as a hostage until His work was completely fulfilled. That ful-fillment was proclaimed when He came forth from His contemptible imprisonment, and His coming forth be-came our justification: "[He] *was raised again for our justification*" (v. 25). If Jesus had not fully paid the debt,

He would have remained in the grave. If He had not made conclusive, total, final atonement, He would have continued to be a captive. But He had done it all. The *"It is finished"* (John 19:30) that came from His own lips was established by the verdict of Jehovah, and Jesus was set free.

Beloved, let us rejoice in this. In the empty tomb of Christ, sin has been put away forever; therefore, death has also been destroyed most effectively. Our sins were the great stone that shut the mouth of the sepulcher and held us captive in death and darkness and despair. Like the stone, our sins have now been rolled away forever, and death is no longer a dark and dreary dungeon, the waiting room of hell. Instead, it is a perfumed bedroom, a sitting room, the waiting room of heaven. For as surely as Jesus rose, His people must also be made alive. There is nothing to prevent the resurrection of believers. The stone that could keep us in the prison has been rolled away. Who can lock us in when the door itself is gone? Who can confine us when every barricade has been taken away?

> Who shall rebuild for the tyrant his prison?
> The scepter lies broken that fell from his hands;
> The stone is removed; the Lord is arisen:
> The helpless shall soon be released from their bands.

A Trophy Displayed

Secondly, we should regard the stone as a trophy. Men in ancient times set up memorial stones, and today we erect monuments to tell of great deeds of heroism. Similarly, the stone that was rolled away was, as it were, consecrated that day before the eyes of our faith as a

11

memorial of Christ's eternal victory over the powers of
death and hell. These powers thought that they had vanquished Him; they believed that the Crucified One had
been overcome. They smiled grimly when they saw His
motionless body wrapped in grave clothes and placed in
Joseph's new tomb. However, their joy was fleeting, their
boasting was only very brief, for, at the appointed moment, He who could not see corruption (Psalm 49:9) rose
and came forth from beneath their power. His heel had
been bruised by the old Serpent, but on the morning of
the Resurrection, He crushed the Dragon's head
(Genesis 3:15).

> Vain the stone, the watch, the seal,
> Christ has burst the gates of hell;
> Death in vain forbids Him rise,
> Christ has open'd Paradise.
>
> Lives again our glorious King!
> "Where, O death, is now thy sting?"
> Once He died our souls to save;
> "Where's thy victory, boasting grave?"

Beloved in Christ, as we look at the stone with the
angel seated upon it, it rises before us as a monument of
Christ's victory over death and hell, and it is appropriate
for us to remember that His victory was achieved for us
and that the fruits of it are all ours. We have to fight
against sin, but Christ has overcome sin. We are tempted
by Satan, yet Christ has defeated our Enemy. We eventually will leave our bodies; unless the Lord comes soon,
we may expect to yield our spirits and be *"gathered unto
[our] people"* (Genesis 49:33), like Jacob, and go to meet
our God. But death has been vanquished for us, and
there is no reason for us to fear.

The Stone Rolled Away

Have courage, Christian soldier; you are encountering a vanquished enemy. Remember that the Lord's victory guarantees yours. If the Head conquers, the members of the body will not be defeated. Do not let tears blur your eyes; do not let fears trouble your spirit. You will conquer, for Christ has conquered. Awaken all your faculties to the conflict, and strengthen them with the hope of victory. Place that stone before the eye of your faith right now, and say, "Here my Master conquered death and hell, and in His name and by His strength I will be crowned a victor, too, when the last enemy is destroyed."

A Foundation Laid

Next, observe that a foundation is laid here. The stone that was rolled away from the sepulcher both typifies and certifies the resurrection of Jesus Christ; it is a foundation stone for faith in Christ. The fact of the Resurrection is the keystone of Christianity. If the resurrection of our Lord were to be disproved, our holy faith would be a mere fable. There would be nothing for faith to rest upon if He who died upon the cross did not also rise again from the tomb. As the apostle Paul said, if this were the case, *"your faith is* [in] *vain; ye are yet in your sins"* (1 Corinthians 15:17), while *"they also which are fallen asleep in Christ are perished"* (v. 18). All the great doctrines of our faith would fall away like the stones of an arch if the keystone were to be dislodged; they would be toppled together in a heap of rubble, for all of our hope hinges upon that great fact. If Jesus rose, then this Gospel is what it professes to be. If He did not rise from the dead, then it is all deceit and delusion.

However, the fact that Jesus rose from the dead is a truth that has been established better than any other fact in history. There were many witnesses; they were men of all classes and conditions in life. None of them ever confessed that they had been mistaken or that they had deceived anyone. They were so persuaded that it was the truth that most of them suffered death for bearing witness to it. They had nothing to gain by such testimony; they did not rise in power or gain honor or wealth. They were truthful, guileless men who testified what they had seen and bore witness to what they had observed.

Again, the Resurrection is a fact that is better attested than any other event recorded in history, whether ancient or modern. This is the confidence we can have as believers: our Lord Jesus Christ—who made a good confession before Pontius Pilate (1 Timothy 6:13) and who was crucified, dead, and buried—rose again from the dead and after forty days ascended to the throne of God. We rest in Him; we believe in Him. If He has not risen, *"we are of all men most miserable"* (1 Corinthians 15:19) to be His followers. If He has not risen, His atonement has not proven to be sufficient. If He has not risen, His blood has not proven to be effective in removing our sin. However, since He has risen, we build upon this truth. We rest all our confidence upon it, and we are persuaded that,

> Raised from the dead, He goes before;
> He opens heaven's eternal door;
> To give His saints a blest abode,
> Near their Redeemer and their God.

My dear reader, are you resting your everlasting hopes on the resurrection of Jesus Christ from the dead? Are you trusting in Him, believing that He both died and rose again for you? Are you depending entirely on the merit of His blood, which has been certified by the fact that He rose again?

If so, you have built on a foundation of fact and truth, a foundation against which the gates of hell will not prevail. However, if you are building on anything that you have done, or anything that a priest can do for you, you are building on sand, which will be swept away by the all-devouring flood, and you and your hopes will go down into the fathomless abyss, wrapped in the darkness of despair. Oh, if you will build on the *"living stone"* (1 Peter 2:4) of Christ Jesus and rest on Him who is a proven cornerstone, *"chosen...and precious"* (v. 4), you will build safely, eternally, and blessedly!

A Rest Provided

The fourth truth about the stone is that rest is provided. The angel seemed to teach us this when he sat down upon the stone. How leisurely the whole Resurrection was effected! How noiselessly, too! What an absence of fanfare and parade! The angel descended, the stone was rolled away, Christ rose, and then the angel sat down on the stone. He sat there silently and gracefully, breathing defiance to the Jews and their seal, to the Roman legionnaires and their spears, to death, to earth, to hell. He as good as said, "Come and try to roll that stone back again, you enemies of the Risen One. All you infernal powers who tried to prevail against our ever living Prince, roll back that stone again, if you dare or can!"

The angel did not say this in words, but the very stately and quiet way in which he sat upon the stone meant all that and more. The Master's work is done, and done forever. This stone, which is to be used no more—this unhinged door, which is no longer to be used to seal off death's house—is one of which we may say, *"It is finished"* (John 19:30): finished so that it can never be undone, finished so that it will remain that way eternally. The angel softly whispers to us, "Come here, and rest." There is no fuller, better, surer, safer rest for a person than in the fact that the Savior in whom he trusts has risen from the dead.

Are you mourning your departed friends? I urge you to come and sit upon this stone, which tells you that they will rise again. Do you expect to die soon? Do you show signs of terminal illness? Please come and sit down upon this stone, and remember that death has lost its terror now, for Jesus has risen from the tomb. Come, you who are feeble and trembling, and breathe defiance to death and hell. The angel will vacate his seat for you and let you sit down in the face of these enemies. Even if you think you are insignificant, or if you are broken and pale and weak through long years of weary sickness, you may still defy the hosts of hell very well, while you rest upon this precious truth: *"He is not here: for he is risen"* (Matthew 28:6). He has left the land of the dead and will never die again.

> Every note with wonders swell,
> Sin o'erthrown, and captived hell;
> Where is hell's once dreaded king?
> Where, O death, thy mortal sting?
> Hallelujah!

An Appointed Boundary

Fifthly, the stone is an appointed boundary. Do you not recognize that it is? Look at it, then. There it lies, and the angel sits upon it. On the one side, what do you see? There are the frightened guards, stiffened like dead men because of their fear. On the other side, what do you see? There are the timid, trembling women, to whom the angel softly speaks, *"Fear not ye: for I know that ye seek Jesus"* (Matthew 28:5). You see, then, that the stone became the boundary between the dead and the living, between the haters of Christ and the seekers of Christ, between His enemies and His friends. To His enemies, His resurrection is *"a stone of stumbling and...a rock of offence"* (Isaiah 8:14). They mock it, just as the Athenian philosophers on Mars' Hill mocked Paul when the apostle spoke to them of the Resurrection (Acts 17:22–32). But to Christ's own people, the Resurrection is the cornerstone of faith and life. Our Lord's resurrection is our triumph and delight.

The Resurrection functions in much the same manner as did the pillar that Jehovah placed between Israel and Egypt: it was darkness to Egypt, but it gave light to Israel. All was dark amid Egypt's armies, but all was brightness and comfort among Israel's tribes. So the Resurrection is a doctrine full of horror to those who do not know and trust Christ. What do they have to gain by resurrection? Oh, the horrors of that tremendous morning when every sinner will rise and the risen Savior will come in the clouds of heaven with all His holy angels (Matthew 24:30–31)! Truly there is nothing but dismay for those who are on the evil side of that resurrection stone.

But how great is the joy that the Resurrection brings to those who are on the right side of that stone! They look for His appearing with an ecstasy that grows daily. They build upon the delightful truth that they will rise and see their Savior with their own eyes. I want you to ask yourself on which side of that boundary stone you are now. Do you have life in Christ? Are you risen with

Christ? Are you trusting only in Him who rose from the dead? If so, do not fear; the angel comforts you, and Jesus reassures you. However, if you do not have life in Christ, but are dead while you live, let the very thought that Jesus is risen strike you with fear and make you tremble, for you may well tremble at what awaits you.

A Foreshadowing of Ruin

Lastly, I believe that this stone may very legitimately be seen as a foreshadowing of ruin. Our Lord came into this world to destroy all the works of the Devil. Imagine the works of the Devil as a grim and horrible castle: massive and terrible, overgrown with the moss of ages, colossal, cemented with the blood of men, fortified by devilry and deceit, surrounded with deep trenches, and garrisoned with demons. This is a structure frightening enough to cause despair to everyone who circles around it in order to count its towers and its bulwarks.

Yet, in the fullness of time (Galatians 4:4), our Champion came into the world to destroy the works of the Devil. During His life on earth, He sounded an alarm at the great castle and dislodged a stone here and there: the sick were healed, the dead were raised, and the poor had the Gospel preached to them (Luke 7:22). But on the morning of the Resurrection, the enormous fortress trembled from top to bottom; huge cracks appeared in its walls, and all its strongholds were tottering. One who is stronger than the master of that fortress (Luke 11:22) had evidently entered it and was beginning to *"overturn, overturn, overturn"* (Ezekiel 21:27) it, from pinnacle to basement. One huge stone, upon which the building greatly depended—a cornerstone that held the whole structure together—was lifted bodily from the foundation and was hurled to the ground.

Jesus tore the huge granite stone of death from its position, and, in doing so, He gave a sure sign that every other stone would follow. When that stone was rolled away from Jesus' sepulcher, it was a prophecy that every stone of Satan's building would come down and that, of all the stones that the powers of darkness had ever piled up, from the days of their first apostasy to the end, not one stone would rest upon another. (See Mark 13:2.)

My friend, the stone that was rolled away from the door of the tomb gives me glorious hope. Evil is still mighty, but evil will be brought down. Spiritual wickedness reigns in high places (Ephesians 6:12); the multitudes still clamor after evil (Exodus 23:2); the nations still sit in thick darkness (Isaiah 42:6–7); many worship the scarlet woman of Babylon (Revelation 17:3–5); others bow before the religion of Islam, and millions worship blocks of wood and stone (Deuteronomy 29:17); the dark places and habitations of the earth are still full of cruelty (Psalm 74:20). However, you can be sure that Christ has shaken the whole structure of evil so powerfully that every stone will be certain to fall.

We must just continue to work, to use the battering ram of the Gospel, to hold our positions, and, like the armies around Jericho, to persist in sounding the trumpet, for the day will come when every age-old evil, every colossal superstition, will be laid low, as low as the ground. Then this prophecy will be fulfilled: *"Overturn, overturn, overturn, it: and it shall be no more, until he come whose right it is; and I will give it him"* (Ezekiel 21:27). That loosened stone on which the angel sits is the sure prophecy of the coming doom of everything that is base and vile. Rejoice, you sons of God, for Babylon's fall will soon come. Sing, O heavens, and rejoice, O earth, for not one evil will be spared. I tell you the truth, *"there shall not be left one stone upon another, that shall not be thrown down"* (Mark 13:2).

Now that we have heard the message of the stone, let us hear what the angel has to say.

THE MESSAGE OF THE ANGEL

The angel preached in two ways: he preached in symbols, and he preached in words.

The Gospel of Symbols

Note well that the angel was a symbolic preacher, with his countenance of lightning and his robe of snow (Matthew 28:3). However, please recognize for whom the symbols were reserved. He did not say a word to the guards—not a word. He gave them the symbolic Gospel; that is, he looked upon them, and his glance was as lightning. He revealed himself to them in his snow-white garments and in no other way. Note how they shook and trembled! That is the Gospel of symbols, and wherever it comes, it condemns. It can do nothing else.

In contrast to the symbolic Gospel, what did the old Mosaic Law of symbols result in? How few ever discovered its inner meaning! The majority of the people of Israel fell into idolatry, and the symbolic system became death to them. We see the same thing today in the institutionalized church. Preaching in symbols is very popular with certain religious groups nowadays. The Gospel is to be seen by the eye, they tell us, and the people are to learn by seeing a change of colors at various seasons, such as blue and green and violet, exhibited on the priest and the altar, and by lace and candles and banners and goblets and shells full of water. The people are even to be taught through their sense of smell, which is to be indulged with the smoke of incense, and by their sense of hearing, through hideous chanting or delicate canticles.

However, the gospel message is, *"Incline your ear, and come unto me: hear, and your soul shall live"* (Isaiah 55:3). This is the life-giving message: *"Believe on the Lord Jesus Christ, and thou shalt be saved"* (Acts 16:31). *"An evil and adulterous generation seeketh after a sign"* (Matthew 12:39), and if you look for symbols and signs, you will be deluded with the Devil's gospel and fall prey to the Destroyer.

The Gospel of Words and Thoughts

Now let us listen to the words of the angel's message. Only in this way may the true Gospel be delivered. Christ is the Word, and the Gospel is a Gospel of words and thoughts. It does not appeal to the eye; it appeals to the intellect and to the heart. It is a spiritual thing, and it can only be learned by those whose spirits are awake to spiritual truth.

The first thing the angel said was, *"Fear not ye"* (Matthew 28:5). This is the very character of our risen Savior's Gospel: *"Fear not ye."* You who desire to be saved, you who want to follow Christ, you do not need to fear. Did the earth quake at the Resurrection? Do not fear. God can preserve you, even if the earth should be burned with fire. Did the angel descend in frightening majesty? Do not fear; there are no terrors in heaven for the child of God who comes to Jesus' cross and trusts his spirit to Him who bled there. Is it the dark that alarms you? Do not fear; God sees and loves you in the dark, and there is nothing in the dark or in the light that is beyond His control.

Are you afraid to approach a tomb? Does a sepulcher alarm you? Do not fear; you cannot die. Since Christ has risen, *"though* [you] *were dead, yet shall* [you] *live"* (John 11:25). Oh, the comfort of the Gospel! Permit me to say that there is nothing in the Bible to make any man fear who puts his trust in Jesus. Nothing in the Bible? Why, there is nothing in heaven, nothing on earth, nothing in hell that can make you fear if you have put your trust in Jesus. *"Fear not ye."*

You do not need to fear the past; you are forgiven for it. You do not need to fear the present; it is provided for. The future is also secured by the living power of Jesus. He said, *"Because I live, ye shall live also"* (John 14:19). Shall we fear? Fear was proper and appropriate when Christ was dead, but now that He lives there is no place for it! Do you fear your sins? They are all gone, for Christ would not have risen if He had not done away with them.

What is it that you fear? If an angel tells you, *"Fear not,"* why do you continue to fear? If every wound of the risen Savior and every act of your reigning Lord console you, why are you still dismayed? To doubt and fear and tremble, now that Jesus has risen, is an inconsistent thing in any believer. Jesus is able to deliver you in all your temptations. *"He is able also to save* [you] *to the uttermost...seeing he ever liveth to make intercession for* [you]*"* (Hebrews 7:25); therefore, do not fear.

Notice the words that follow: *"Fear not ye: for I know"* (Matthew 28:5). What? Did the angel know the women's hearts? Did the angel know what Mary Magdalene thought and felt? Do angelic beings read our spirits? It is possible. However, it is far better to remember that our heavenly Father knows. Do not fear, for God knows what is in your heart.

Perhaps you have never acknowledged that you are
anxious about where you will spend eternity; you are too
timid even for that. You have not even gone so far as to
dare to say that you hope you love Jesus, but God knows
your desires. Poor heart, you feel as if you could not trust
in Him and could not do anything that is good. Yet, you
do at least desire Him; you do at least seek Him. God
knows all this; He spies out your desires with pleasure.
"Fear not ye," for your heavenly Father knows. Lie still,
poor patient, for the Surgeon knows where the wound is
and what it is that ails you. Hush, my child, sit still on
your great Parent's lap, for He knows everything. His
care is as infinite as His knowledge. Should you not be
content with that?

The angel went on to say, *"Fear not ye: for I know
that ye seek Jesus, which was crucified"* (Matthew 28:5).
There was a need for comfort here. The women were
seeking Jesus, though the world had crucified Him. Even
though the majority had turned aside and left Him, they
were clinging to Him in loving loyalty. Now, can you say,
"Though I am unworthy to be a follower of Christ, and
often think that He will reject me, there is still one thing
I am sure of—I would not be afraid of man for His sake.
My sins make me fear, but no man could do it. I would
stand at His side if the whole world were against Him. I
would consider it my highest honor that the Crucified
One of the world should be the adored One of my heart.
Even if the whole world should cast Him out, if He would
just take me in, poor unworthy worm that I am, I would
never be ashamed to acknowledge His blessed and gracious name." If you can say that, then do not fear, for if
that is how you feel about Christ, He will acknowledge
you in the Last Great Day (Matthew 10:32). If you are
willing to confess Him now, *"Fear not ye."*

Jesus Rose for You

Then the angel added, *"He is not here: for he is risen"* (Matthew 28:6). After giving comfort, he gave instruction. Your great basis and reason for hope, if you are seeking Christ, is that you do not seek a dead Jesus and you do not pray to a buried Savior; He is really alive. He is as able to help you today, if you pray to Him, as He was to help the poor blind man when He was on earth. He is as willing today to accept and bless you as He was to bless the leper or to heal the paralytic. Therefore, dear seeker, go to Him at once. Go to Him with holy confidence, for He is no longer in the tomb—He would be dead if He were—but He is risen, living, and reigning and He will answer your request.

The angel instructed the women to investigate the empty tomb, but almost immediately afterward, he gave them a commission to perform on their Lord's behalf: *"Go quickly, and tell his disciples that he is risen from the dead"* (Matthew 28:7). Now, if you have been seeking Christ and have been comforted by the thought that Christ lives to intercede for you and is able to save you to the uttermost (Hebrews 7:25), and if you have trusted Christ, then do as the angel said. Go and tell others of the good news that you have heard. I urge you not to keep the blessed secret to yourself. Today, in some way or other, I pray that you will make it known that Jesus Christ is risen. Pass the saying around, as the ancient Christians did. On the first day of the week, they said to one another, *"The Lord is risen indeed"* (Luke 24:34).

If anyone asks you what you mean by this, you will then be able to tell them the entire Gospel, for this is its essence: Jesus Christ died for our sins and rose again on the third day, according to the Scriptures (1 Corinthians 15:3–4). He died as our Substitute, for we were criminals; He rose as our Representative, for we are now pardoned

The Stone Rolled Away

sinners. He died so that our sins might die, and He lives again so that our spirits may live.

Diligently invite others to trust Jesus. Tell them that the spiritually dead may receive life with just one look at the crucified Jesus. Tell them that this look is a matter of the soul; it is simple trust in Him. Tell them that no one who has trusted in Christ has ever been cast away. Tell them what you have felt as the result of your trusting Jesus. Perhaps many disciples will be added to His church, a risen Savior will be further glorified, and you will be comforted by what you have seen! I pray that the Lord will compensate for my inadequate words with His own blessing, for Christ's sake.

Chapter Two

A Visit to the Tomb

*He is not here: for he is risen, as he said. Come, see
the place where the Lord lay.*
—Matthew 28:6

A s we saw in the first chapter, Mary Magdalene
and the other Mary came to the sepulcher hoping
to find the body of their Lord, which they intended to embalm. Their intention was good, their will
was accepted before God, but, even so, their desire was
not gratified, for the simple reason that it was contrary
to God's plan. It was even at variance with what Christ
had predicted and had plainly declared to them. The angel told them, *"He is not here: for he is risen, as he said."*
I conclude from this that, as believers, we may have good
desires in our hearts and we may earnestly try to carry
them out, and yet we may never succeed in them because
through our ignorance we have not understood—or
through our forgetfulness we may have failed to remember—some vital word of Christ that prevents them.

I have known this to be the case regarding prayer.
We have prayed and we have not received because we
have had no basis in the Word of God for our particular
requests. Perhaps there are some prohibitions in the

Scriptures that restrain us from offering these prayers. In our daily lives, amid the pursuits of business, we have thought that if we could gain such and such a position, then we would honor God. Yet, although we have sought it vigorously and prayed about it earnestly, we have never gained it. Perhaps God never intended that we should gain it, and if we had succeeded in securing our own plan, it might have been bad for us rather than something advantageous, an inheritance of trouble instead of a heritage of joy.

We may have been seeking great things for ourselves, forgetting the admonishment of the Lord, *"Seekest thou great things for thyself? seek them not"* (Jeremiah 45:5). Do not, therefore, expect to attain all those desires that seem to you to be pure and proper. They may not happen to run in the right channel. It may be that there is a word from the Lord that forbids you from ever seeing them come to pass.

The two women who approached the tomb of Jesus found that they had lost the presence of Him who had been their greatest delight. *"He is not here"* must have sounded to them like the sad tolling of a church bell at a funeral. They expected to find Him, yet He was gone. But then the grief must have been taken out of their hearts when the angel added, *"He is risen."* I gather from this that if God takes away from me any good thing, He will be sure to justify Himself in having done so, and very frequently He will glorify His grace by giving me something infinitely better.

Did Mary think it would be a good thing to find the dead body of her Lord? Perhaps it would have given her a kind of melancholy satisfaction. It appears that she thought so in her limited judgment. The Lord took that "good thing" away from Mary. But then she learned that

A Visit to the Tomb

Christ was risen; and for Mary first to hear of His resurrection and then shortly to see Him, was that not an infinitely better thing?

Have you lost anything lately around which your heart had intertwined all its hopes? You will find that there is a good reason for the loss. The Lord never takes away a silver blessing without intending to give us something golden. Depend upon it: for wood He will give iron, and for iron He will give brass, and for brass He will give silver, and for silver He will give gold. Everything He takes is but the preliminary to His giving us something greater.

Perhaps you have you lost a precious child. Even in this difficult circumstance, the Lord may become more dear to you than ever. One smile of your Lord will be better to you than even the cheerful antics of your child. Is He not better to you than ten sons? (1 Samuel 1:8). Have you lost the familiar companion who once cheered you along the valley of life? You will now by that loss be driven closer to your Savior; His promises will be sweeter to you, and the Blessed Spirit will reveal His truth to you more clearly. You will gain by your loss.

"He is not here"—that is sorrowful. But, *"He is risen"*—that is joyful. You cannot see the dead Christ. You cannot tenderly embalm that blessed body. But you will see Christ, the Living One; at His feet you will be able to prostrate yourself, and from His lips you will hear the joyful words, "Go, tell my brothers that I have risen from the dead" (Matthew 28:7, 10).

That lesson may be worth remembering. If God applies it to your soul, it may yield rich comfort for you. Again, if the Lord takes away one joy from you, He will give you another and a better one. *"He doth not afflict willingly nor grieve the children of men"* (Lamentations

3:33). I am sure that you never deny your children any good pleasure without intending their real good. After requiring your children to exercise a little self-denial, you probably have a way of making it up to them again so that they do not lose anything by it. And your heavenly Father will deal quite as gently and tenderly with you as His child.

With these comforting thoughts, that God knows what is best for us and is working all things together for our good, let us now explore our text more closely. We will see that, though Christ's crucifixion looked like defeat at first, God fulfilled His plan of redemption by raising Christ from the dead. Our text illustrates our hope of redemption by first giving us an assurance, *"He is not here: for he is risen,"* and secondly, by extending to us an invitation, *"Come, see the place where the Lord lay."*

AN ASSURANCE

Jesus Christ has really risen from the dead. As I wrote earlier, there is probably no fact in history that is so fully proven and corroborated as the fact that Jesus of Nazareth, who was nailed to the cross, who died and was buried, also rose again. We believe the histories of Julius Caesar, we accept the statements of Tacitus, the Roman historian, and we are bound, on the same grounds, to accept the written testimonies of Matthew, Mark, Luke, and John as historical documents and to accept the testimony of those who were eyewitnesses of His death and who saw Him after He had risen from the dead.

Jesus Christ rose from the dead. This is not an allegory or a symbol, but a reality. He lay dead—a fact that both His friends and enemies were able to witness—a corpse fit to be committed to the grave. If you had been there, you could have easily handled Him and seen this. He would have been the very Christ you knew in life, the very same.

Imagine that you were there. Look into those eyes. Were there ever such eyes in any other human being? Look at Him! You can see the imprint of sorrow on His face. Was there ever any countenance as marred as His, any sorrow as real in its effects as His? This is the Emperor of misery, the Prince of all mourners, the King of sorrow! There He lies, unmistakably the same. Now, note the nail prints. There is where the nails went through those blessed hands, and there is where His feet were pierced. There is the gash from the Roman soldier's spear that went all the way through to the sac that enclosed His heart and tore it, bringing forth that amazing blood and water from His side (John 19:34). It is He, the same Christ! You can see the women lift each limb and wrap Him in linen and put the spices around Him—as much as they had brought in their haste. You can see them lay Him in that new tomb.

Now, let it be known and understood that I believe that those very limbs that lay stiff and cold in death became warm with life again, that the very body that lay there became infused with life again and came forth into a glorious existence. His hands took the piece of honeycomb and the fish in the presence of the disciples, and with His mouth He ate them (Luke 24:42–43). He held out those wounds and said, *"Reach hither thy finger, and behold my hands"* (John 20:27), and He showed His side, the same side that was pierced, and said, *"Reach hither thy hand, and thrust it into my side: and be not faithless, but believing"* (v. 27). He was no phantom, no ghost. As He Himself said, *"A spirit hath not flesh and bones, as ye see me have"* (Luke 24:39). He was truly human, as much after the Resurrection as He had been before; and He is truly human in glory now, even as He was when He was here below. He has gone up; the cloud has received Him out of our sight.

He is the same Christ who said to Peter, *"Lovest thou me?"* (John 21:15), the same Jesus who said to His disciples, *"Come and dine"* (v. 12)—a real man has really risen from a real death into a real life. Now, we always need to have that doctrine stated to us plainly, for although we believe it, we do not always fully comprehend it, and even if we have comprehended it, it is good to hear it again, in order to confirm it in our minds. The Resurrection is as literal a fact as any other fact stated in history, and it is to be believed as such by us. *"He is not here: for he is risen."*

Follow the biblical narrative, beloved, and you will see that when our Lord Jesus Christ had risen, having been quickened from the state of death, it was true not only that He had really risen from the sepulcher, but also that He had risen in order to ascend to a higher place. He now possesses the position of glory at the right hand of the Father. After He had burst the iron shackles of the grave, the disciples had this for their consolation: He was now beyond the reach of His enemies. They could no longer hurt Him. And that is still true today.

Therefore, *"He is not here"* in another sense. He is now beyond the reach of all His evil adversaries. Does this encourage you? It encourages me. No Judas can now betray the Master so that He is seized by Roman guards. No Pilate can now take Him and subvert justice and hand Him over to be crucified, even though he knows that He is innocent. No Herod can now mock Him with his soldiers; no soldiers can now spit in His dear face. No one can now beat Him or blindfold Him and say to Him, *"Prophesy unto us, thou Christ, Who is he that smote thee?"* (Matthew 26:68). The head, the dear, majestic head of Jesus, can never again be crowned with thorns, and the busy feet that ran errands of mercy can never again be pierced by nails. Men will no longer strip Him naked and then stand and exult over His agonies. He has gone beyond their reach.

Now His enemies may rail at Him and seek to spite Him through His people, who are the members of His body. Now they may rage; but God has set Jesus at His own right hand, and He is inaccessible to their malice. Oh, blessed are the following words, blessed was the pen that wrote them, and blessed was the Spirit who dictated them:

> *Wherefore God also hath highly exalted him, and given him a name which is above every name: that at the name of Jesus every knee should bow, of things in heaven, and things in earth, and things under the earth; and that every tongue should confess that Jesus Christ is Lord, to the glory of God the Father.*   *(Philippians 2:9–11)*

It should comfort us to think that our Lord is now beyond all pain, as well as beyond all personal attack. Oh, can you bear to think that He did not have anywhere to lay His head (Matthew 8:20)? Would we not have given up our beds to have given Him a night's rest? More than that, would we not have renounced our beds forever if we might have given Him a soft place on which to lie down? Would we not have slept on a hillside all night, until our heads were wet with dew, if we could have provided rest for Him?

He is worth ten thousand of us. Does it not seem as if it was too much for Him to have had to suffer in that way—to be without a home or even a shelter? My friend, He was hungry, He was thirsty, He was weary, He was faint. He suffered our sicknesses; we are told that He took them upon Himself. He often had heartache. He knew how the cold mountains and the midnight air could chill the body. And He knew how a bleak atmosphere and bitter loss could freeze the soul. He passed through innumerable griefs and sorrows.

From the first shedding of blood at His birth (Matthew 2:16), down to the last shedding of blood at His death, it seemed as if sorrow had marked Him as a special child. He was always troubled, tempted, disquieted, assailed, assaulted, and harassed by Satan, by wicked men, and by the evils of the world around him. Yet, now He is not subject to any of that, and for that reason we are glad that He is not here.

Our Lord is no child of poverty now; there is no carpenter's shop for Him now. He no longer has to wear the one-piece garment of the peasant, *"woven from the top throughout"* (John 19:23). He no longer has to use the mountainside for His bed. There are no jeering crowds around Him now; no one picks up rocks to stone Him now. He does not have to sit wearily on a well, saying, *"Give me to drink"* (John 4:7); He does not need to be supplied with food when He is hungry. There is no more scourging and whipping for Him. No longer will He give "[His] *back to the smiters, and* [His] *cheeks to them that plucked off the hair"* (Isaiah 50:6). No one is piercing His hands and His feet now; He is not enduring burning thirst upon the bloody cross. He no longer has to cry out, *"My God, my God, why hast thou forsaken me?"* (Mark 15:34).

A Visit to the Tomb

God's waves and billows went over Him once, but they can assail Him no more. At one time He was brought into the dust of death, and His soul was exceedingly sorrowful. Yet He is beyond all that. Now the raging sea has passed, and He has come to the fair haven where no storms can beat upon Him. He has reached His joy, He has entered into His rest, and He has received His reward. Beloved, let us be glad about this. Let us enter into the joy of our Lord. Let us be glad because He is glad; let us be happy because He is happy. Oh, that we might feel our hearts leaping within us—even though for a little while longer we are on the field of battle— because He is completely gone from it and is now acknowledged and adored as King of Kings and Lord of Lords.

Not only does the fact that our Lord has risen have these comforting elements about it, with reference to Him, but it is also the guarantee, to every one of us who believes in Him, of our own resurrection. In his first epistle to the Corinthians, the apostle Paul made the whole argument for the resurrection of the body hinge upon this one question: Did Christ rise from the dead? If He did, then all His people must rise with Him. He was the representative Man, and since the Lord and Savior rose, all His followers must rise also. Once you have settled the question that Christ rose, you have settled the question that all who are in Him, and who are conformed to His image, must rise, too.

The body of that dear believer to whom you said goodbye some years ago will rise again. Those eyes that were closed in death—those very eyes—*"shall see the king in his beauty* [in] *the land that is very far off"* (Isaiah 33:17). Those ears that could not hear you when you spoke your last tender words of farewell—those ears will hear the eternal melodies. That heart that grew stone cold and still, when Death laid his cold hand upon the chest of your dear friend, will beat again with newness of life. It will leap with joy amid the festivities of the homecoming, when Christ, the Bridegroom, will be married to His church, the bride.

All this will happen to that same body! Was it not the temple of the Holy Spirit? Was it not redeemed with blood? Surely it will rise at *"the voice of the archangel, and...the trump of God"* (1 Thessalonians 4:16)! Be sure of this, be sure of it—sure for your friend and sure for yourself. And do not fear death, for what is death? The grave is but a bath in which our body buries itself in spices, like Esther did, to make it sweet and fresh for the embrace of the glorious King in immortality. (See Esther 2:8–9, 12.) It is but the closet where we put aside our garments for a while. They will come out cleansed and purified, with many golden decorations on them that were not there before. They were our work clothes when we took them off; they will be our Sunday best when we put them on, and they will be appropriate for Sabbath wear. We may even long for evening to come so that we may undress, if there is to be such a waking and such a putting on of garments in the presence of the King.

Further, let us remember that there is another comforting thought in the fact that our Lord is not here but has risen. He has gone where He can best protect our interests. He is an advocate for us (1 John 2:1). Where should the Advocate be but in the King's court? He is preparing a place for us (John 14:2–3). Where should the One who is preparing a place for us be but there, making it ready? We have a very active Adversary, who is busy accusing us. Is it not a good thing that we have One who can meet our Enemy face-to-face and put *"the accuser of* [the] *brethren"* (Revelation 12:10) to silence? It would be precious to have Him here, but He is more precious there. He is doing more for us in heaven than it could have been possible for Him to do for us here below, as far as our finite intelligence can judge, and as truly as His infinite wisdom has pronounced.

Meanwhile, we are well compensated for His absence by the presence of His own Spirit (John 16:7), and His presence in heaven is well consecrated by His personal administration of sacred service for our sake. All is well in heaven, for Jesus is there. The crown is safe, and the harp is secure; and the blessed heritage of each tribe of Israel is entirely secure, for Christ is keeping it. He is, to the glory of God, the Representative and Preserver of His people.

And does this truth, that Christ is not here but is gone, not fall upon our ears with a sweet force as it compels us to feel that this is the reason why our hearts should not be here? Since *"He is not here,"* then our hearts should not be here. When this text, *"He is not here,"* was first spoken, it meant that He was not in the grave. He was somewhere on earth then. But now He no longer lives here in the flesh; He has gone into heaven.

Suppose you are very rich, and Satan whispers to you, "You live in a stately mansion, surrounded by delightful gardens. You can take it easy." You should reply to him, "But He is not here; He has risen. Therefore, I do not dare to put my heart where my Lord no longer is." Or, suppose your family makes you very happy, and as the little ones cluster around you and you all sit together in front of a cozy fire, your heart is very glad. Though you do not have much of this world's goods, you have enough, and you have a contented mind. Well, if Satan should say to you, "Be well content, and take your rest here," say to him, "No, *'He is not here,'* and I cannot feel that this is to be my place of rest. Only where Jesus is can my spirit rest."

Have you just started out in life? Have you recently been married? Are you just now beginning the happy days of youth, the sweet enchantment of this life's purest joy? Well, delight in this, but still remember that *"He is not here,"* and therefore you have no right to say to yourself, "You can take it easy!" Christ is nowhere on earth, and therefore there is nowhere on earth that your heart may build its nest. Let your soul rise up to God, and let all your sweetest incense go toward Him who *"is not here: for he is risen."*

AN INVITATION

Secondly, our text includes an invitation: *"Come, see the place where the Lord lay."*

I am not going to say much about Joseph of Arimathea's tomb, for I think any tomb might suffice to point out the same sacred truth. In a little town in Italy, I once got a vivid picture of what the tomb of Christ must have been like, in something that had been built for Catholic pilgrims. I was up on the hillside, and I saw these words written on a wall in Latin: "And there was a garden." I pushed open the door to this garden. It was like any other garden, but the moment I entered I saw a marker in the shape of a hand, with the words, "And in the garden there was a new tomb." Then I saw a tomb that had been newly painted, and when I came up to it I read these words that were written on it: "A new tomb in which no man had ever lain." I then stooped down to look inside the tomb, and I read the inscription, which was written in Latin: "Stooping down, he looked, yet he

38

did not go in." But these words were also written there: "Come, see the place where the Lord lay." I went in, and I saw, engraved in stone, the napkin and the linen clothes lying by themselves. The words, "He is not here, for he is risen," were engraved on the floor of the tomb.

Though I dislike anything stagy and theatrical, I certainly greatly envisioned the reality of the scene through this experience. I felt that Jesus Christ had really been buried, really laid in the earth, and that He has really gone out of the world. It is good for us to come and see the place where Jesus lay.

Why should we see it? Well, first, so that we may see how remarkably humble Jesus was to ever have lain in the grave. He who made heaven and earth, lay in the grave. He who gave light to angels' eyes, lay in the darkness for three days. He slept in the darkness there. He, without whom *was not any thing made that was made"* (John 1:3), was given up to death and lay a victim of death in the grave. Oh, wonder of wonders! Marvel of marvels! He who had life and immortality within Himself yielded Himself up to the place of death!

Next, *"come, see the place where the Lord lay,"* in order to see how we ought to weep over the sin that laid Him there. Did I make the Savior lie in the grave? Was it necessary that before my sin could be put away, my sweet Prince, whose beauties enchant all heaven, had to be stiff and cold in death, and actually be laid in the tomb? Did it have to be so? Oh, you murderous sins! You murderous sins! You cruel and cursed sins! Did you slay my Savior? Did you cause that tender heart to die? Could you never be content until you had led Him to His death and laid Him there? Oh, beloved, come and weep as you see the place where the Lord lay.

"Come, see the place where the Lord lay," so that you may see where you will have to lie, unless the Lord suddenly returns. You may check the dimensions of that grave, for that is where you will have to rest. It does us good to remember, even if we have great wealth and property, that six feet of earth is all that will ever be our permanent estate. We will have to come to it—that solitary mound, consisting of about two yards of level ground:

> Princes, this clay must be your bed,
> In spite of all your towers;
> The tall, the wise, the reverent head
> Must lie as low as ours.

There is no alternative to this. To the dust we must all return. Therefore, come in order to see that you must lie there, too.

But then, *"Come, see the place where the Lord lay,"* so that you may also see what good company you will have there. That is where Jesus lay; does that thought not comfort you?

> Why should the Christian fear the day
> That lands him in the tomb;
> There the dear flesh of Jesus lay,
> And left a long perfume.

What is a more appropriate chamber for a prince's son to go to sleep in than the prince's own tomb? Immanuel slept in the grave, and there, my body, you may be well content to sleep, too! What more royal bed can you desire than in the arms of the same mother earth in which the Savior was laid to rest for a while? Think, beloved, of the thousands of believers who have gone that way to heaven. Who can dread going where all the flock have gone? You poor, timid sheep, if you alone had to go through this dark valley, you might well be afraid; but in addition to your Shepherd, who marches at the head of all the flock, there are innumerable sheep that follow Him. Some were very dear to you and fed in the same pasture with you. Do you dread going where they have gone? No; see the place where Jesus lay, in order to see what good company is to be had there, even though it may seem to be in a dark chamber.

"Come, see the place where the Lord lay," in order to see that you will not lie there long. It is not the place where Jesus is now. He is gone, and you are to be with Him where He is. Come, and look at this tomb. There is no door to it. There was one; it was a huge rock, a monstrous stone, and no one could move it. It was sealed. Remember how they sealed the stone, setting the stamp of the Sanhedrin, the stamp of the law, upon it, to make it secure so that no one could move it?

But now, go to the place where Jesus lay, and see that the seal has been broken, the guards have fled, the stone is gone. This is the way your tomb will be. It is true that they will cover you up and shovel sod over your grave. If you are wise, you will prefer this to the heavy slabs of stone they sometimes lay upon the graves of the dead. You will sleep in that sweet mound of earth, and it will have a daisy here and there, like the eyes of earth looking up to heaven asking for mercy or smiling in the joy of expectation.

Yet, remember this: in the morning, when you wake up, don't you simply open your eyes, get up, pull back the curtains, and come out of your house to do the work of the day with no one standing in your way? Similarly, when the trumpet of the Resurrection sounds, you will rise out of your bed in perfect freedom, with no one hindering you, and you will see the light of the day that will never again turn to night. There will be nothing to confine you. There will be no bolt or bar, no guard or watchman, no stone and seal—nothing. Come, see the place where Jesus lay. I would not want to go to bed in a prison in which there was a guard to lock me in with his iron key. But I am not afraid to go to sleep in the chamber out of which I can come in the morning as a perfectly free man! And it will be the same with you, beloved, if you are a believer. You will come to lie in a place that is open and free—a place that is fit for the Lord's freemen to sleep.

"Come, see the place where the Lord lay," in order to celebrate His triumph over death. If Miriam sang at the Red Sea, we also may sing at Jesus' tomb. If she said, *"Sing ye to the LORD, for he hath triumphed gloriously"* (Exodus 15:21), will we not say the same? If all the multitudes of Israel joined with her in this song, the women with dances and the strong men with their voices, let all God's people go forth today, in the same way, and bless and praise the Lord, saying, *"O death, where is thy sting? O grave, where is thy victory?"* (1 Corinthians 15:55). The place where Jesus lay has told us,

> Vain the watch, the stone, the seal!
> Christ has burst the gates of hell.

Let us sing to Him and give Him all the praise.

Let us come and see the place where Jesus lay, in order to weep there for our sins; let us come and see the place where Jesus lay, in order to die there to our sins; let us come and see the place where Jesus lay, so that we may be buried there with Him. Let us come so that we may rise from that place to newness of life and find our way through the resurrection life into the ascension life. Then we will sit in the heavenly place and look down upon the things of earth with joyous contempt, knowing that He has lifted us far above them and made us partakers of brighter bliss than this earth can ever know.

I pray that you will share in this. You already have a share in dying. There is a tree growing, out of which your coffin will be made; or perhaps it has already been cut down and is seasoning in preparation for the time when it will be made into a suit of timber for you—the last suit that you will ever need. There is a spot of earth that must be shoveled out for you to be laid into. But your spirit will live; your spirit will never die. Do not for a moment believe those who tell you that you will be annihilated at death. Your spirit will still exist.

Moreover, your body will be raised either to life or to damnation. Ask yourself the hard question of whether you will spend eternity in hell *"where* [the] *worm dieth not, and the fire is not quenched"* (Mark 9:44), or with Christ, who lives in His glory and who will come a second time to give glory to His people and raise their bodies like His own (Romans 8:11).

Oh, it will all hinge on this: Do you believe in Jesus? If you do, you may welcome life and death and resurrection and immortality. But if you do not believe, then a catastrophe has come upon you, and to you it is terrible to die. It is terrible even to live, but more terrible to die; it will be terrible to rise again; it will be terrible to be damned forever! God save you from it, for Christ's sake!

Chapter Three

Christ, the Destroyer of Death

The last enemy that shall be destroyed is death.
—1 Corinthians 15:26

What a wonderful Savior we have, who has died and been resurrected for us so that we may live eternally! As we have seen, one of man's greatest enemies is death. The inevitability of death robs us of peace and causes us to despair or to live lives devoid of purpose. Death is a formidable enemy, but Christ has won the victory. Christ is the destroyer of death! This is one of the Redeemer's greatest characteristics. May the Spirit of God lead us into a full understanding of the tremendous victory over death that Christ has won for us.

Our text teaches us three important truths about this great foe: death is an enemy, death is an enemy that will be destroyed, and death is the enemy that will be destroyed last.

DEATH IS AN ENEMY

First, death is truly an enemy. It was born that way, even as Haman the Agagite was the enemy of Israel because of his ancestry (Esther 3:1–10). Death is the child of our worst enemy, for *"sin, when it is finished, bringeth forth death"* (James 1:15). Remember, *"Sin entered into the world, and death by sin"* (Romans 5:12). Now, that which is distinctly the fruit of transgression cannot be anything but an enemy to man. Death was introduced into the world on that gloomy day on which man fell, and our archenemy and betrayer, the Devil, had the power of it. From both of these facts, we must regard death as the clear enemy of man.

Death is an alien in this world; it did not enter into the original design of the unfallen creation, but its intrusion marred and spoiled the whole thing. It does not belong to the Great Shepherd's flock, but it is a wolf that comes to kill and to destroy.

Geologists tell us that there was death among the various forms of life from the first ages of the globe's history, even when the world had not yet been fashioned as the dwelling of man. I can believe this and still regard death as the result of sin. If it can be proven that there is such an organic unity between man and the lower animals that they would not have died if Adam had not sinned, then I see in those deaths before Adam the consequences of a sin that was as yet uncommitted. By the merits of Jesus, there was salvation before He had offered His atoning sacrifice, and I do not find it hard to believe that the foreseen offenses of sin may have cast the shadow of death over the long ages that came before man's transgression.

We know only a little about what occurred at the beginnings of creation, and it is not important that we should, but as far as this present creation is concerned, it is certain that death is not God's invited guest but an intruder whose presence mars the feast. Man, in his foolishness, welcomed Satan and sin when they forced their way into Paradise, but he never welcomed death; even his blind eyes could see a cruel enemy in that skeleton form. Death is to the sons of men as the lion is to the herds of the plain, as the sickle is to the flowers of the field, as the wind is to the dry leaves of the forest. They fear it by an inward instinct because their consciences tell them that it is the child of their sin.

Death is well described as an enemy, for it does an enemy's work toward us. Why does an enemy come except to root up and to pull down and to destroy? Death tears in pieces that beautiful handiwork of God—the fabric of the human body that has been so marvelously sewn by the fingers of divine skill. By casting this rich embroidery into the grave among the armies of the worm, death gives to its fierce soldiers *"a prey of divers colours, a prey of divers colours of needlework"* (Judges 5:30), and they ruthlessly tear the plunder in pieces.

Borrowing from the language of the twelfth chapter of Ecclesiastes, this building of the human body is a house that is beautiful to look upon, but Death destroys it. It darkens its windows, shakes its pillars, closes its doors, and stops the musicians from playing. Then the daughters of music sing faintly, and the strong men stoop. This vandal spares no work of life, however full of wisdom or beauty it may be; Death severs the silver cord and breaks the golden bowl. Look—at the fountain the costly pitcher has been utterly broken, and at the well the well-crafted wheel has been dashed in pieces. (See Ecclesiastes 12:3–6.)

Death is a fierce invader of the realms of life, and where it comes it cuts down every good tree, stops up all wells of water, and mars every good piece of land with stones. Have you seen a man when death has worked its will upon him? What a ruin he is! His beauty is turned to ashes and his handsome features to decay. Surely an enemy has done this.

My friend, look at the course of death throughout all ages and in all lands. Is there any field without its grave? What city is there without its cemetery? Where can we go to find no sepulchers? As the sandy shore is covered with the shells of sea life, so is the earth covered with those small, grass-covered hills beneath which sleep the departed generations of men. Even the sea is not without its dead! As if the earth were all too full of corpses and they jostled each other in their crowded sepulchers, into the caverns of the mighty ocean the bodies of the dead are cast. Its waves must be defiled with the carcasses of men, and on its floor must lie the bones of the slain!

Our enemy, death, has marched, as it were, with sword and fire, ravaging the human race. Neither the Goths nor the Huns nor the Tartars could have slain so universally all who breathed, for death has allowed none to escape. Everywhere it has withered the joy of families and created sorrow and sighing. In all lands where the sun is seen, it has blinded men's eyes with weeping. The tears of the bereaved, the grieving of the widow, and the moans of the orphan—these have been death's war music, its songs of victory.

The greatest conquerors have only been death's slaughterers, butcher tradesmen working in its slaughterhouse. War is nothing more than death holding a carnival and devouring its prey a little faster than it is commonly accustomed to.

Death has also done the work of an enemy to those of us who have as yet escaped its arrows. Those who have recently stood around a newly made grave and buried half their hearts can tell you what an enemy death is. It takes friends from our sides and children from our homes, and it is unconcerned about our crying. It topples the man who was the pillar of his household, and it snatches away the mother who was the brightness of the home. The little one is torn out of his mother's arms, though his loss almost breaks her heart, and the blossoming youth is taken from his father's side, though the parent's fondest hopes are now crushed.

Death has no pity for the young and no mercy for the old; it pays no regard to the good or the beautiful. Its sickle cuts down sweet flowers and harmful weeds with equal readiness. It comes into our gardens, tramples down our lilies, and scatters our roses on the ground. Yes, death spies out even the most modest flowers that have been planted in the corner and that hide their beauty beneath the leaves so that they may blush unseen; it cares nothing for their fragrance but withers them with its burning breath. Death is your enemy, indeed, you fatherless child; you have been left for the pitiless storm of a cruel world to beat upon, with no one to shelter you. Death is your enemy, poor widow, for the light of your life is gone and the desire of your eyes has been removed with a single blow. Death is your enemy, husband, for your house is desolate and your little children cry for the mother whom death has robbed.

Even those who die may well consider death to be their enemy. I do not mean once they have risen to their heavenly home, and, as disembodied spirits, behold the King in His beauty. Rather, death is their enemy before that, while it is approaching them. Death seems to their trembling flesh to be a foe, for it is not natural, except in moments of extreme pain or unsoundness of mind or of excessive expectation of glory, for us to be in love with death. It was wise of our Creator to make us in such as way that the spirit loves the body and the body loves the spirit, and that they desire to dwell together as long as they can. Otherwise, people would not care about self-preservation, and suicide would have destroyed the human race by now.

When death comes even to the good man, it comes as an enemy, for it is attended by terrible messengers and grim escorts in the form of illnesses that greatly scare us. None of the illnesses that afflict us adds a particle of beauty to the appearance of death. Death comes with pains and grief; it comes with sighs and tears. Clouds and darkness are around it, an atmosphere weighted with dust oppresses those whom it approaches, and a cold wind chills them right to the marrow of their bones. Death rides on the pale horse (Revelation 6:8), and where his steed sets its feet, the land becomes a desert. By the hoofbeat of that terrifying steed, the worm is awakened to gnaw the slain. When we forget other great truths and only remember these dreadful things, death is the king of terrors to us. Hearts are sickened and restraints are loosened because of death.

A Common Enemy

If you think for a few moments about this enemy, you will note some of the aspects of its character. It is the common foe of all God's people and the enemy of all men. No matter how much some people have been persuaded that they would not die, there no discharge in this war that death wages against us. Moreover, even if a man escapes being drafted into this war for many years until his gray beard seems to defy the winter's hardest frost, this man of iron must yield in the end. *"It is appointed unto men once to die"* (Hebrews 9:27). The strongest man has no access to a fountain of youth with which he may renew his youthfulness amid the decay of aging and have eternal life. Nor has the wealthiest prince a price with which he may bribe destruction. Crowned monarchs cannot escape the grave, either, for there is not a large difference between a scepter and a shovel. In former times, even powerful and noble knights have had to go down to the sepulcher, for sword and spade are made of similar metals. The prince is brother to the worm and must dwell in the same house. Of our whole race it is true, *"Dust thou art, and unto dust shalt thou return"* (Genesis 3:19).

A Subtle Enemy

Death is also a subtle enemy, lurking everywhere, even in the most harmless things. Who can tell where death has not prepared its ambushes? It meets us both at home and abroad; it attacks men in their food, and it poisons their drink. It waylays us in the streets and seizes us in our beds; it rides on the storms at sea and walks with us when we are making our way on solid ground. Where can we run to escape from you, O Death, for from the summit of the Alps men have fallen to their graves, and in the deep places of the earth, where the miner goes down to find valuable ore, you have sacrificed many precious lives. You are a subtle foe, and with noiseless footsteps you follow close at our heels when we least think of you.

Death is an enemy none of us will be able to avoid, no matter what side roads we may take. Nor can we escape from it when our hour has come. Like birds, we will all fly into this poacher's net; all the fishes of the great sea of life must be taken in its great net when their day has come. As surely as the sun sets or as the midnight stars eventually descend beneath the horizon or as the waves sink back into the sea or as the bubble bursts, we must all sooner or later come to our end and disappear from earth, to be known no more among the living.

A Sudden Enemy

In addition, the assaults of this enemy are often sudden.

> Leaves have their time to fall,
>   And flowers to wither at the north wind's breath,
> And stars to set—but all,
>   Thou hast all seasons for thine own, O Death!

Men have died without more than an instant's notice; with a psalm on their lips, they have passed away. Or, while they have been engaged in daily business, they have been summoned to give their account. I heard of one man who, when the morning paper brought him the news that a friend in business had died, was putting on his shoes to go to his office. He observed with a laugh that as far as he was concerned, he was so busy that he had no time to die. Yet, before the words were finished, he fell forward and was a corpse. Sudden deaths are not so uncommon that they are astonishing to us, especially if we live in a place where there are a large number of people. Therefore, death is not a foe to scorn or to trifle with. If we remember all its characteristics, we will not be inclined to think lightly of the grim enemy whom our glorious Redeemer has destroyed.

DEATH IS AN ENEMY TO BE DESTROYED

Secondly, let us remember that death is an enemy that will be destroyed. Remember that our Lord Jesus

Christ has already won a great victory over death and has delivered us from lifelong bondage to our fear of death (Hebrews 2:15). He has not yet destroyed death, but He has come very close to it, for we are told that He has *"abolished death, and hath brought life and immortality to light through the gospel"* (2 Timothy 1:10). This surely must be very close to destroying death altogether.

Let us look more carefully at how Christ has already conquered death and how He will destroy it completely in the end.

Christ Delivered Us from Spiritual Death

In the first place, our Lord has subdued death in the very highest sense by delivering His people from spiritual death. *"And you hath he quickened, who were dead in trespasses and sins"* (Ephesians 2:1). At one time you had no divine life whatsoever; the death of original sin and depravity remained upon you, and so you were dead to all divine and spiritual things. But now, beloved, the Spirit of God who raised Jesus Christ from the dead has raised you into newness of life, and you have become a new creation in Christ Jesus. In this sense, death has been subdued.

Christ Raised the Dead

When He was on earth, our Lord also conquered death by restoring certain individuals to life. There were three memorable cases in which, at Christ's command, the last enemy gave up its prey. Our Lord went into the ruler of the synagogue's house and saw the little girl who had just fallen asleep in death, around whom everyone was weeping and mourning (Luke 8:49–52). He heard the scornful laughter when He said, *"She is not dead, but sleepeth"* (v. 52), and He made them all leave and said to her, *"Maid, arise"* (v. 54). Then the plunderer was plundered, and the dungeon door was opened.

Jesus also stopped the funeral procession at the gates of Nain, where they were carrying out a young man, *"the only son of his mother, and she was a widow"* (Luke 7:12). Jesus said, *"Young man, I say unto thee, Arise"* (v. 14). When that young man sat up and our Lord presented him to his mother, the prey was again taken from mighty Death.

In the greatest example, Lazarus had lain in the grave so long that his sister said, *"Lord, by this time he stinketh"* (John 11:39). However, in obedience to the words, *"Lazarus, come forth"* (v. 43), the raised one came out with his grave clothes still around him, yet fully alive. At that moment, death was recognized as subservient to the Son of Man. *"Loose him, and let him go"* (v. 44), said the conquering Christ, and death's chains were removed, for the lawful captive was delivered. When, at the Redeemer's resurrection, many of the saints arose and came out of their graves into the holy city (Matthew 27:50–53), then the crucified Lord was proclaimed to be victorious over death and the grave.

Christ Suffered the Penalty of Death

Still, beloved, these were but foreshadowings and preliminary skirmishes of the glorious victory by which death was overthrown. The real triumph was achieved upon the cross.

When Christ died, He suffered the penalty of death on behalf of all His people, and therefore no believer dies as a punishment for sin, since we cannot dream that a righteous God would twice exact the penalty for one offense. Death is not a penal infliction upon the children of God. As a form of punishment, Christ has abolished death, and it can never be enforced. Why do believers die, then? It is because their bodies must be changed before they can enter heaven.

"Flesh and blood," in their present form, *"cannot inherit the kingdom of God"* (1 Corinthians 15:50). A divine change must take place upon the body before it will be fit for incorruptibility and glory, and death and the grave are, as it were, the refining pot and the furnace by which the body is made ready for its future bliss. It is true that death is not yet destroyed, but our living Redeemer has changed it so much that it is no longer death, but something else! Believers do not now die, but they are dissolved and then they depart. It is as if death detaches the cable so that the ship may freely sail to the fair havens. Death is the fiery chariot in which we ascend to God; it is the gentle voice of the Great King who comes into His banqueting hall and says, *"Friend, go up higher"* (Luke 14:10). Behold, on eagles' wings we mount, we fly, far from this land of mist and cloud, into the eternal serenity and brilliance of God's own house above. Yes, our Lord has abolished death. *"The sting of death is sin"* (1 Corinthians 15:56), but our great Substitute has taken that sting away by His great sacrifice. Stingless, death remains among the people of God, but it harms them so little that to them it is not death to die.

Christ Rose from the Dead Triumphantly

Further, Christ vanquished death and thoroughly overcame it when He rose. It is tempting for me to paint a full picture of the Resurrection for you right now, but I will not be diverted from my main point more than to apply a few brushstrokes to the portrait.

When our great Champion awoke from His brief sleep of death and found Himself in the waiting room of the grave, He quietly proceeded to put aside the garments of the tomb. How leisurely He proceeded! He folded up the napkin and placed it by itself (John 20:7), so that those who lose their friends might wipe their eyes with it. Then He took off the grave clothes and laid them by themselves (v. 6), so that they might be there when His saints follow Him to the grave, so that the chamber might be well furnished and the bed might be made and prepared for their rest.

The sepulcher is no longer an empty vault, a dreary mausoleum, but a chamber of rest, a dormitory furnished and prepared, hung with the tapestry that Christ Himself has bequeathed. It is no longer a damp, dark, dreary prison; Jesus has changed all that.

> 'Tis now a cell where angels use
> To come and go with heavenly news.

The angel from heaven rolled away the stone from our Lord's sepulcher and let in fresh air and light upon Him again; He stepped out more than a conqueror (Romans 8:37). Death had fled. The grave had capitulated.

> Lives again our glorious King!
> "Where, O death, is now thy sting?"
> Once He died our souls to save;
> "Where's thy victory, boasting grave?"

Christ, the Destroyer of Death

Christ's Resurrection Guarantees Ours

Well, beloved, as surely as Christ rose, He guaranteed, as an absolute certainty, the resurrection of the bodies of all His children into a glorious life; the life of their spirits never pauses even for a moment. He conquered death with His resurrection, and since that memorable victory, Christ has been overcoming death every day, for He gives His Spirit to His people. Because they have His Spirit within them, they meet the last enemy without alarm. They often confront him with songs; perhaps more frequently they face him with calmness and fall asleep with peace.

I will not fear you, death; why should I? You look like a dragon, but your sting is gone. Your teeth are broken, old lion; why should I fear you? I know that you are no longer able to destroy me but that you are sent as a messenger to conduct me to the golden gate through which I will enter and see my Savior's unveiled face forever. Dying believers have often said that their last beds have been the best they have ever slept upon. Many of them have inquired, "Tell me, my soul, can this be death?"

Dying has been so different an experience from what they expected it to be, so cheerful and so joyful, and they have been so free of all care, have felt so relieved instead of burdened, that they have wondered whether this could be the monster they had been so afraid of all their lives. They find it to be like a pinprick, whereas they feared it would be like the deep wound of a sword. It is the shutting of one's eyes on earth and the opening of them in heaven, whereas they had thought it would be like being stretched on the rack or like a dreary passage through a dismal region of gloom and dread. Beloved, our exalted Lord has overcome death in all these ways.

DEATH WILL BE DESTROYED LAST

But note that this is not the meaning of the text—the text speaks of something yet to be done. The last enemy that *"shall be"* destroyed is death, so that death in the sense meant by the text has not yet been destroyed. It is to be destroyed in the future. How will this happen?

Well, I understand the text to mean that death will be destroyed last in several different ways.

Those Who Are Alive Will Not See Death

The first meaning implied by the text is that, at the coming of Christ, those *"which are alive and remain"* (1 Thessalonians 4:17) will not see death; they *"shall be changed"* (1 Corinthians 15:52). Even the living must undergo a change before they can inherit eternal life, but they will not actually die. The multitude of the Lord's own who will be alive at His coming will pass into glory without needing to die. Thus, death, as far as they are concerned, will be destroyed.

But as for the sleeping ones, the myriads who have left their flesh and bones to decay back to dust, death will be destroyed even in regard to them, for when the trumpet sounds, they will rise from the tomb. The Resurrection is the destruction of death. I have never taught or believed or thought that every particle of every body that is put into the grave will be reunited with the spirit and that the absolutely identical material will rise. However, I do say that the identical body will be raised, as surely as seed that is put into the ground comes out of it again. It will be in a very different form, for a seed does not come forth again as a seed but as a flower; nevertheless, the same body will surely rise again.

Christop# Christ, the Destroyer of Death

It is not necessary that a body be raised with the same material; yet, out of the grave, or out of the earth if it never saw a grave, or out of the ocean if it was drowned and consumed by the creatures of the sea, will come the same body that corresponds to a person's true identity, that was inhabited by his spirit while it was here below. Was it not so with our Lord? It will be the same way with His own people, and then the Scripture will be fulfilled: *"Death is swallowed up in victory. O death, where is thy sting? O grave, where is thy victory?"* (1 Corinthians 15:54–55).

We Will Not Be Worse Off for Having Died

There will be another feature in our Lord's victory: death will be fully destroyed because those who rise will not be one bit the worse for having died. I believe that upon those new bodies there will be no trace of the feebleness of old age, no indications of a long and wearying sickness, none of the scars of martyrdom. Death will not have left its mark upon them at all, unless it is some mark of glory that will be to their honor, like the scars in the flesh of the Well Beloved. Even now, His scars are His chief beauty in the eyes of those for whom His hands and feet were pierced. In this sense, death will be destroyed because it will have done no damage to believers at all; every trace of decay will have been swept away from the redeemed.

There Will Be No More Death at All

And then, finally, after this trumpet of the Lord, *"there shall be no more death, neither sorrow, nor crying, neither shall there be any more pain: for the former things are passed away"* (Revelation 21:4).

"Christ being raised from the dead dieth no more; death hath no more dominion over him" (Romans 6:9). Therefore, the quickened ones, His own redeemed, will also never again die. Oh, it is a dreadful, dreadful supposition to think that they should ever have to undergo temptation or pain or death a second time. It cannot be. Christ says, *"Because I live, ye shall live also"* (John 14:19).

As the doctrine of the immortality of the soul has been given up by some, a number of these people have felt obliged to give up the concept of an eternity of future punishment along with the concept of an eternity of future bliss. Assuredly, as far as some great proof texts are concerned, they stand or fall together: *"These shall go away into everlasting punishment: but the righteous into life eternal"* (Matthew 25:46). If one eternal state is short, the other must be also; whatever the adjective *everlasting* means in one case, it means in the other. To believers, the word means endless duration in both cases; we look forward to a bliss that will never come to an end. It is then, in that tearless, sorrowless, graveless country that death will be utterly destroyed.

Death Is Our Last Enemy

And now, last of all—and the word *last* seems very appropriate in this context—death is to be destroyed last. Because it came in last, it must go out last. Death was not the first of our enemies: first came the Devil, then sin, then death. Death is not the worst of enemies; death is an enemy, but it is much to be preferred over our other adversaries. It would be better to die a thousand times than to sin. To be tried by death is nothing compared with being tempted by the Devil. The mere physical pains connected with death are trivial compared with the hideous grief that is caused by sin and the burden that a sense of guilt causes to the soul. Death is but a secondary evil compared with the defilement of sin. Let the great enemies go down first: *"Smite the shepherd, and the sheep shall be scattered"* (Mark 14:27). Let sin, and Satan, the lord of all these evils, be struck down first, and death may well be left to the last.

Notice that death is the last enemy of each individual Christian, and the last to be destroyed. Well now, if the Word of God says it is the last, I want to give you a little piece of practical wisdom—allow it to be the last. Do not dispute the appointed order, but let the last be last.

I knew a brother in Christ who wanted to conquer death long before he died. But you do not need dying grace until your dying moments. What would be the good of dying grace while you are still alive? A boat is only necessary when you reach a river. Ask for living grace, and glorify Christ with it, and then you will have dying grace when the time for death comes. Your enemy is going to be destroyed, but not today. There is a great multitude of enemies to be fought today, and you may be content to let this one alone for a while.

This enemy will be destroyed, but of *"the times or the seasons"* we are in ignorance (Acts 1:7). It is wise for us to be good soldiers of Jesus Christ, as the duty of every day requires. Take your trials as they come, child of God. In due time, God will help you to overcome the world, the flesh, and the Devil. If you live well, you will die well. The same covenant through which the Lord Jesus gave you life, also contains the grant of death, *"for all things are yours; whether...life, or death, or things present, or things to come; all are yours; and ye are Christ's; and Christ is God's"* (1 Corinthians 3:21–23).

Why is death left to the last? Well, I think it is because Christ can make much use of it. *The last enemy that shall be destroyed is death,* because death has been and will be of great service before it is destroyed. Oh, what lessons some of us have learned from death! There are, perhaps, no sermons like the deaths that have happened in our own households; the departures of our beloved friends have been to us like solemn discourses of divine wisdom, which our hearts could not help hearing. So Christ has spared death to make it a preacher to His redeemed ones.

If I may die as I have seen some of my church members die, I welcome the grand occasion. I would not wish to escape death by some shortcut, if I may sing as they sang. If I may have the hosannas and hallelujahs beaming in my own eyes that I have seen and heard from them, it would be a blessed thing to die. Yes, as a supreme test of love and faith, it is a good thing for death to be given a respite for a while, in order to allow the redeemed to glorify their Master in it.

Besides, beloved, without death we would perhaps not be as conformed to Christ as we will be if we fall asleep in Him. There will not be any jealousy in heaven among the redeemed; however, I almost think that any believer who does not die, but is changed when Christ comes, could meet you and me, who probably will die, and say, "My brother, my sister, there is one thing I have missed. I never lay in the grave. Death never laid its cold hand on me, and so in this I was not conformed to my Lord. But you know what it is to have fellowship with Him even in His death." Is it not true that those who are alive and remain when Christ comes will have no preference over those who fall asleep? I think the preference, if there is one, will belong to us who sleep in Jesus and wake up in His likeness.

Death, dear friends, has not yet been destroyed, because it brings God's children home. It merely comes to them and whispers its message, and in a moment they are supremely blessed.

> Have done with sin and care and woe,
> And with the Savior rest.

And so, death is not destroyed yet, for it serves useful purposes. But, beloved, it is going to be destroyed. It is the last enemy of the church as a whole. The church as a body has had a large number of foes to contend with, but after the Resurrection we will say, "This is the last enemy. Not another foe is left." Eternity will roll on in ceaseless bliss. There may be changes that bring new delights; perhaps in the eternity to come there may be eras and ages of yet more amazing bliss and still more superlative ecstasy, but there will be

> No rude alarm of raging foes,
> No cares to break the last repose.

The last enemy that will be destroyed is death, and if the last enemy is slain, there can be no future foe. The battle has been fought and the victory has been won forever. And who has won it? Who but the Lamb that sits on the throne? Let us give Him honor and glory and majesty and power and dominion and might, forever and ever. May the Lord help us in our solemn adoration.

Chapter Four

Great Truths of the Resurrection

Remember that Jesus Christ of the seed of David was
raised from the dead according to my gospel.
—2 Timothy 2:8

I n Paul's second letter to Timothy, from which our
text is taken, we see that the esteemed apostle was
anxious about the young man who had preached with
remarkable success, and whom he regarded in some respects as his successor. The old man was about to put off
his *"tabernacle"* (2 Corinthians 5:1), and he was concerned that his son in the Gospel should preach the same
truth as his father has preached and should by no means
adulterate the Gospel.

There was a tendency in the days of the early
church, and the same tendency exists today, to try to get
away from the simple matters of fact upon which Christianity has been built, to something more philosophical
and hard to understand. Often, the word that the common people hear gladly is not fine enough for cultured
scholars, and so they must surround it with a mist of
human thought and speculation.

Three or four plain facts constitute the Gospel. Paul
outlined them in the fifteenth chapter of his first epistle
to the Corinthians:

Jesus Rose for You

*For I delivered unto you first of all that which I
also received, how that Christ died for our sins according to the scriptures; and that he was buried,
and that he rose again the third day according to
the scriptures.*   *(1 Corinthians 15:3–4)*

Our salvation hinges upon the incarnation, life, death,
and resurrection of Jesus. He who truly believes these
truths has believed the Gospel, and through believing
the Gospel he will without doubt find eternal salvation.

However, men want novelties; they cannot stand the
fact that a trumpet always makes exactly the same
sound; they crave some fresh improvisation every day.
The Gospel with variations is the music they like. Intellect is progressive, they say. Therefore, they must march
ahead of their forefathers. Incarnate Deity, a holy life, an
atoning death, and a literal resurrection—having heard
these things now for nearly two thousand years, they are
just a little stale, and the cultivated mind hungers for a
change from the old-fashioned manna. Even in Paul's
day, this tendency was manifest, and so they sought to
regard facts as mysteries or parables. They tried to find a
spiritual meaning in them until they went so far as to
deny them as actual facts. The apostle Paul was very
anxious that Timothy, at least, should stand firm with
the original testimony of the Gospel and should understand in its plain meaning Paul's witness to the fact that
"Jesus Christ of the seed of David" rose again from the
dead.

Within our text, several facts are recorded. First,
there is the great truth that Jesus, the Son of the Highest,
was anointed of God. The apostle called Him *"Christ,"*
that is, the Anointed One, the Messiah, the One sent by
God. He also called Him *"Jesus,"* which signifies a savior,

and it is a magnificent truth that He who was born of Mary, He who was laid in the manger at Bethlehem, He who loved and lived and died for us, is the ordained and anointed Savior of men. We do not have a moment's doubt about the mission, office, and purpose of our Lord Jesus; in fact, the salvation of our souls hangs upon the fact that He was anointed by the Lord God to be the Savior of men.

This Jesus Christ was really and truly man, for Paul said He was *"of the seed of David."* True, He was divine, and His birth was not an ordinary one, but in all respects He still shared our human nature and came from the line of David. This we also believe. We are not among those who spiritualize the Incarnation and suppose that God was here as a spirit or that the whole story is only an instructive legend. No, in real flesh and blood the Son of God lived among men. He was bone of our bone and flesh of our flesh in the days of His sojourn here below. We know and believe that Jesus Christ has come in the flesh (1 John 4:2). We love the Incarnate God, and we place our trust in Him.

The text also implies that Jesus truly died, for He could not be raised from the dead if He had not first gone down among the dead and been one of them. Yes, Jesus died. The Crucifixion was no delusion; the piercing of His side with a spear was very clear and evident proof that He was dead. His heart was pierced, and the blood and water flowed from it (John 19:33–34). As a dead man, He was taken down from the cross, carried by gentle hands, and laid in Joseph's new tomb.

Imagine that pale corpse, as white as a lily. Notice how it is stained with the blood of His five wounds, blood as red as the rose. See how Joseph and Nicodemus carefully wrap Him in fine linen with sweet spices and leave Him to spend His Sabbath all alone in the rock-hewn sepulcher. *"He made his grave with the wicked, and with the rich in his death"* (Isaiah 53:9). No man in this world was ever more surely dead than He. As one who was dead, they laid Him in the place of the dead, with a cloth around his head and grave clothes and garments fit for a grave. Then they rolled the great stone against the mouth of the tomb and left Him, knowing that He was dead.

Then comes the wonderful truth that as soon as the sun began its shining circuit on the third day, Jesus rose again. His body had not decayed, for it was not possible for the Holy One to experience corruption (Psalm 16:10). However, His body had still been dead, and by the power of God—by Jesus' own power, by the Father's power, by the power of the Spirit, for the Scriptures attribute it to each of these in turn—before the sun had risen His dead body was quickened. His silent heart began to beat again, and through the stagnant canals of His veins the blood began to flow and circulate. The Redeemer's spirit took possession of His body again, and it lived once more. There He was inside the sepulcher, as truly alive in all the members of His body as He had ever been. He literally and truly, in a material body, came forth from the tomb, and He lived among men until the hour of His ascension into heaven.

This is the truth that is still to be taught, no matter who tries to refine it, no matter who dares to spiritualize it. This is the historical fact that the apostles witnessed; this is the truth for which the confessors of the faith bled and died. This is the doctrine that is the keystone of the arch of Christianity, and they who do not hold it have cast aside the essential truth of God. How can they hope for salvation for their souls if they do not believe that *"the Lord is risen indeed"* (Luke 24:34)?

68

Great Truths of the Resurrection

Now let us look at some of the implications of the resurrection of Jesus Christ. First, what does the Resurrection prove regarding Christ and who He claimed to be? Secondly, what does the Resurrection mean for the Gospel, for our text says, *"Jesus Christ of the seed of David was raised from the dead according to my gospel"*? Thirdly, what implications does this have for us, since our text begins with the word *"remember"*?

WHAT THE RESURRECTION PROVES ABOUT CHRIST

Christ's Claims

Christ's rising from the dead was the seal to all His claims. It was true, then, that He was sent by God, for God raised Him from the dead in confirmation of His mission. Christ Himself had said, *"Destroy this temple* [body], *and in three days I will raise it up"* (John 2:19). And there He was—the temple of His body had been rebuilt! He had even given this as a sign, that as Jonah was three days and three nights in the whale's belly, so would the Son of Man be three days and three nights in the heart of the earth (Matthew 12:39–40) and would then come forth to life again. The sign that He Himself had designated was fulfilled. Before men's eyes, the proof of His claims was clearly evident.

Suppose He had never risen. You and I might have believed in the truth of a certain mission that God had given Him, but we could never have believed in the truth of the commission He claimed to have received—a commission to be our Redeemer from death and hell. How could He be our ransom from the grave if He Himself had remained under the dominion of death?

Christ's Sinlessness

Dear friends, the rising of Christ from the dead proves that this Man was innocent of every sin. He could not be held by the chains of death, for there was no sin to make those chains hold fast. Decay could not touch His pure body, for no original sin had defiled the Holy One. Death could not keep Him a continual prisoner, because He had not actually come under sin. Although He took our sin and bore it as His own, and therefore died, He Himself was sinless; consequently, He had to be set free when the load of sin that had been laid on Him had been removed.

Christ's Deity

Moreover, Christ's rising from the dead proves His claim to deity. We are told in another place that He was proven *"to be the Son of God with power, according to the spirit of holiness, by the resurrection from the dead"* (Romans 1:4). He raised Himself by His own power. The Father and the Holy Spirit participated in the Resurrection, and therefore His resurrection is also attributed to them; however, it was because the Father had granted to Him to have life in Himself (John 5:26) that He rose from the dead.

Oh, Risen Savior, Your rising is the seal of Your work! We can have no doubt about You now that You have left the tomb. Prophet of Nazareth, You are indeed the Christ of God, for God has released You from the chains of death! Son of David, You are indeed the elect and precious One, for You live forever! Your resurrection life has set the signature of heaven to all that You have said and done, and for this we bless and magnify Your name.

Christ's Accepted Sacrifice

The resurrection of our Lord, according to Scripture, was the acceptance of His sacrifice. When the Lord Jesus Christ rose from the dead, this was evidence that He had fully endured the penalty that was due for human guilt. *"The soul that sinneth, it shall die"* (Ezekiel 18:4)—that is the determination of the God of heaven. Jesus stood in the sinner's place and died, and when He had done that, nothing more could be demanded of Him, for He who is dead is free from the law.

Consider a man who has been found guilty of a capital offense. He is sentenced to be hanged, and he is hanged by the neck until he is dead; what more has the law to do with him? It is finished with him, for it has executed its sentence upon him. If he can be brought back to life again, he is clear from the law; the law cannot touch him—he has suffered the penalty.

Therefore, when our Lord Jesus rose from the dead, after having died, He had fully paid the penalty that was due to justice for the sin of His people, and His new life was a life clear of penalty, free from liability. You and I are clear from the claims of the law because Jesus stood in our place, and God will not exact payment both from us and from our Substitute. It would be contrary to justice to sue both the Surety and those for whom He stood. And now, joy upon joy, the burden of liability that once lay upon the Substitute has been removed from Him also, since He has vindicated justice and made satisfaction to the violated law by suffering death. Now, both the sinner and the Surety are free. This is a great joy, a joy that makes the golden harps of heaven ring out with an even more sublime style of music. He who took our debt has now delivered Himself from it by dying on the cross. His new life, now that He has risen from the dead, is a life free from legal claim, and it is the sign to us that we whom He represented are free also.

Take careful note of this: *"Who shall lay any thing to the charge of God's elect? It is God that justifieth. Who is he that condemneth? It is Christ that died, yea rather, that is risen again"* (Romans 8:33–34). It was already a devastating knockdown blow to the Enemy when the apostle said that we cannot be condemned because Christ has died in our place, but he put double force into it when he cried, *"Yea rather, that is risen again."* If Satan, therefore, should come to you and say, "What about your sin?" tell him that Jesus died for it and that your sin has been put away (Hebrews 9:26). If he should come a second time and say to you, "What about your sin?" answer him, "Jesus lives, and His life is the assurance of my justification, for if my Surety had not paid the debt, He would still be under the power of death."

Inasmuch as Jesus has discharged all our liabilities, and left not one penny due to God's justice from one of His people, He lives and is clear from any penalty of the law; and we live in Him and are also clear by virtue of our union with Him. Is this not a glorious doctrine, this doctrine of the Resurrection, as it applies to the justification of the redeemed? The Lord Jesus gave Himself for our sins, but He rose again for our justification (Romans 4:25).

> So Jesus slept: God's dying Son
> Pass'd through the grave, and blest the bed;
> Rest here, dear saint, till from His throne
> The morning break, and pierce the shade.

WHAT THE RESURRECTION SAYS ABOUT THE GOSPEL

Next, the apostle Paul said, *"Jesus Christ...was raised from the dead according to my gospel."* I always like to see in what way any kind of statement bears upon the Gospel. Life is uncertain, and I may not have many more opportunities to preach at my church; therefore, I have made up my mind about this one thing, that I will waste no time on secondary themes, but when I do preach, it will be the Gospel, or something that pertains to it very closely. I will endeavor, each time, like a boxer, to strike under the fifth rib and never beat the air.

In contrast, some preachers remind me of the emperor who excelled only at carving men's heads on small clamshells. What a multitude of preachers we have who can make wonderfully fine discourses out of a mere passing thought, which have no effect on anyone! But we need the Gospel. We have to live and die, and we must have the Gospel. You or I may be cold in our graves in a few weeks, and we cannot afford to toy and trifle with eternal issues. We need to see how all the teachings we hear bear upon our eternal destiny and upon the Gospel that sheds its light over our future.

It Is the Gospel of a Living Savior

First, the resurrection of Christ is vital because it tells us that the Gospel is the Gospel of a living Savior. We do not just send poor repentant sinners to the crucifix, to the dead image of a dead man. We do not say, *"These be thy gods, O Israel"* (Exodus 32:4). We do not send them to a little baby Christ nursed by a woman. Nothing of the sort. We must cause them to look to the Lord *"that liveth, and was dead; and...*[is] *alive for evermore, Amen; and* [has] *the keys of hell and of death"* (Revelation 1:18). He is a living and accessible Savior who still cries out lovingly from the glory of heaven, *"Come unto me, all ye that labour and are heavy laden, and I will give you rest"* (Matthew 11:28). The Scriptures tell us that *"he is able also to save them to the uttermost that come unto God by him, seeing he ever liveth to make intercession for them"* (Hebrews 7:25). We have a living Savior. Is this not a glorious feature of the Gospel?

It Is the Gospel of a Powerful Savior

Notice also that we have a powerful Savior in connection with the Gospel that we preach, for He who had the power to raise Himself from the dead has all power now that He has been raised. He who in death conquered death can conquer even more by His life (Romans 5:10). He who burst all the chains of the grave, even though He Himself was in the grave, can certainly deliver all His people. He who, coming under the power of the law, nevertheless fulfilled the law and thus set His people free from bondage, must be mighty to save. You need a Savior who is strong and mighty, yet you do not need one stronger than He who was *"raised from the dead according to* [the] *gospel."* What a blessed Gospel we have to preach—the Gospel of a living Christ who has Himself returned from the dead, leading captivity captive (Ephesians 4:8).

It Is the Gospel of Complete Justification

Next, we proclaim the Gospel of complete justification. We do not say to people, "Jesus Christ, by His death, did something by which you may be saved if you

74

have a mind to be and if you diligently carry out your good resolves." No, not at all. We say that Jesus Christ took the sin of His people upon Himself and bore the consequences of it in His own body on the cross, so that He died; moreover, having died and therefore paid the penalty, He lives again. Now, all for whom He died, all His people whose sins He bore, are free from the guilt of sin. You ask me, "Who are they?" and I reply, "As many as believe in Him." (See John 1:12.)

Whoever believes in Jesus Christ is as free from the guilt of sin as Christ is. Our Lord Jesus took on Himself the sin of His people and died in the sinner's place. Since He has been set free, all His people have been set free in their Representative. He has performed the work entrusted to Him. He has paid for our transgressions, made an end of sin, and brought in everlasting righteousness; whoever believes in Him is not condemned and never can be.

It Is a Gospel of Eternal Life

In addition, the connection between the Resurrection and the Gospel is that it guarantees the eternal safety of the redeemed. For, if, when Christ rose, His people rose also, they rose to a life that is like their Lord's, and therefore they can never die. It is written, *"Christ being raised from the dead dieth no more; death hath no more dominion over him"* (Romans 6:9). And it is the same with the believer. If you have died with Christ and are risen with Christ, death no longer has dominion over you. You will never go back to the contemptible principles of sin. You will never become what you were before your regeneration. You will never perish, neither will anyone pluck you out of Jesus' hand

75

(John 10:28–29). He has put within you a living and incorruptible seed *"which liveth and abideth for ever"* (1 Peter 1:23). He Himself says, *"The water that I shall give him shall be in him a well of water springing up into everlasting life"* (John 4:14). Therefore, hold fast to this, and let the resurrection of your Lord be your pledge of eternal life.

I cannot describe here all the ways in which the Resurrection relates to the Gospel, but Paul's epistles are filled with them. Paul talked about the Resurrection more than thirty times; he occasionally did so at great length, devoting whole chapters to the glorious theme. The more I think about this theme, the more I delight to preach Jesus and the Resurrection. The good news that Christ is risen is as truly the Gospel as the doctrine that He came to earth and presented His blood as a ransom for men. If angels sang *"Glory to God in the highest"* (Luke 2:14) when the Lord was born, I feel impelled to repeat the song now that He is risen from the dead.

WHAT THE RESURRECTION MEANS FOR US

Now I come to my final point, which is the practical application. What does Christ's resurrection mean for us? To begin with, Paul expressly told us to *"remember"* it. You may be saying, "Well, I haven't forgotten it." Are you sure that you haven't? I find myself far too forgetful of divine truths. We ought not to forget it. The first day of the week has been consecrated to compel us to think of the Resurrection. On the seventh day, the Jewish Sabbath, men celebrated a finished creation. On the first day, Sunday, believers in Christ celebrate a finished redemption. Bear this in mind, then, when you are in church.

Now, if you do remember that *"Jesus Christ of the seed of David"* rose from the dead, what will result from it?

Trials Will Vanish

First, you will find that most of your trials will vanish. Are you distressed by your sin? Jesus Christ rose again from the dead for your justification. Does Satan accuse you? Jesus rose to be your Advocate and Intercessor. Do infirmities hinder you? The living Christ will show Himself strong on your behalf. Do you dread death? In rising again, Jesus has conquered that last enemy of ours. Jesus will come and meet you when it is your turn to pass through the cold stream, and you will cross it in pleasant company. It does not matter what your trouble is, for if you will only think of Jesus as living, full of power, full of love, and full of sympathy, having experienced all your trials, even unto death, you will have such a confidence in His tender care and in His boundless ability that you will follow in His footsteps without question. You have a living Christ, and in Him you have all things. Remember Jesus, and that He rose again from the dead, and your confidence will rise as on eagles' wings.

Sufferings Will Turn to Victory

Next, remember Jesus Himself, for then you will see how your present sufferings are nothing compared to His sufferings, and you will learn to expect victory over your sufferings even as He obtained victory. In the second chapter of 2 Timothy, Paul said, *"Thou therefore endure hardness, as a good soldier of Jesus Christ"* (2 Timothy

2:3). And further on in the chapter, he wrote, *"It is a faithful saying: For if we be dead with him, we shall also live with him: If we suffer, we shall also reign with him"* (vv. 11–12).

Now then, when you are called to suffer, you should think, "Jesus suffered, yet Jesus rose again from the dead. He came up out of His baptism of griefs the better for it, and more glorious as well, and so will I!" Therefore, go into the furnace at the Lord's command, and do not be afraid that the smell of fire will come upon you. Go down even into the grave, and do not think that the worms will make an end of you, any more than they did of Him. See in the Risen One the type and model of what you are to be! Therefore, fear not, for He conquered! Do not stand there trembling, but march boldly on. *"Jesus Christ of the seed of David"* rose from the dead, and you who are of the seed of the promise will rise again from all your trials and afflictions and will live a glorious life.

We see here, dear friends, that in being told to remember Jesus, there is hope even in our hopelessness. When are things most hopeless for a person? Why, when he is dead. Do you know what it is to reach the point of death, as far as your inward weakness is concerned? I do. It takes a great deal to kill us, and it is by being killed that we live. Many people will never live until their proud selves are slain. Sadly, many people are so good and excellent and strong and wise and clever, and all that, that they cannot agree to be saved by grace through faith. If they could be reduced to less than nothing, it would be the finest thing that ever happened to them.

Remember what Solomon said might be done to a fool, and still the fool would not respond? *"Though thou shouldest bray* [grind] *a fool in a mortar among wheat with a pestle, yet will not his foolishness depart from him"* (Proverbs 27:22). That would be rather harsh treatment, and yet his foolishness would not depart from him. The Holy Spirit brings people away from their foolishness not by that process alone, but through a similar method. When He causes them to die to themselves, they may be comforted in the fact that if Jesus Christ literally rose from the dead (not from sickness, but from death), and lives again, His people will also.

Have you ever gotten right under the old dragon's foot, the place where John Bunyan, in his book, *The Pilgrim's Progress,* depicted his character Christian as being? The old dragon, Apollyon, was very heavy, and he pressed the very breath out of a man when he made him his footstool. Poor Christian lay there with the dragon's foot on his chest, but he was just able to stretch out his hand and grasp hold of his sword, which, providentially, lay within his reach. Then he gave Apollyon a deadly thrust, which made him spread his wings and fly away. The poor crushed and broken pilgrim cried out, as he stabbed his foe, "Do not rejoice over me, O my enemy. Though I fall, yet will I rise again." Beloved, do the same. You who are near despair, let this be what strengthens your arm and steels your heart: *"Jesus Christ of the seed of David was raised from the dead according to* [the] *gospel."*

You Will Be Certain of Triumph

Lastly, the Resurrection proves the futility of all opposition to Christ. The learned say they are going to destroy the Christian religion. Already, according to their boasting, it has pretty nearly come to an end. The church has lost its power; it cannot command public attention. Nothing remains for us but to die decently, so they insinuate.

If this is the case, what then? When our Lord was dead, when His cold corpse lay still, guarded by the Roman soldiers, with a seal on the stone, was the cause of Christianity not in mortal jeopardy? But how did it fare? Did it die out? Every disciple that Jesus had made forsook Him and fled. Was Christianity then destroyed? No, that very day our Lord won a victory that shook the gates of hell and caused the universe to stand astonished.

Well, matters have not deteriorated with Him even now. His affairs are not in a worse condition today than they were then. Indeed, see Him today, and judge for yourself. On His head are many crowns, and at His feet the hosts of angels bow! Jesus is the master of legions of men and angels today, while the Caesars have passed away. His people are needy, obscure, despised, I grant you. Still, they are much more numerous than they were when He was laid in the tomb. His cause cannot be crushed; it is forever rising. Year after year, century after century, troops of true and honest hearts continually march up to assault the fortress of Satan.

Truly, if Christ were still dead, I would admit our defeat, for then those who have fallen asleep in Him have perished (1 Corinthians 15:17–18). But since Christ lives, the cause also lives, and those who have fallen asleep are not dead. They have vanished from our sight for a little while, but if the curtain could be drawn, we would see each one of them standing in his destiny unharmed, crowned, victorious! *"What are these which are arrayed in white robes? and whence came they?"* (Revelation 7:13). These are they who were defeated! Then where did their crowns come from? These are they who were dishonored! Then where did their white robes come from? These are they who clung to a cause that has supposedly been overthrown. Then where did the long line of victors come from? There is not a conquered man among them all.

Let the truth be spoken. Defeat is not the word for the cause of Jesus, the Prince of the house of David. We have always been victorious, friends; we are victorious now. Follow your Master on your white horses, and do not be afraid. I see Him in the front with His blood-stained robe around Him, fresh from the winepress where He has trodden down His foes. You yourself do not have to present atoning blood, you only have to follow behind your Lord and conquer. Put on your white garments, and follow Him on your white horse, conquering and going forward to conquer. He is nearer than we think, and the end of all things may come before the next taunt has come out of the mouth of the last new skeptic. Have confidence in the Risen One, and live in the power of His resurrection.

Chapter Five

All Power in Heaven and Earth

And Jesus came and spake unto them, saying, All power is given unto me in heaven and in earth. Go ye therefore, and teach all nations, baptizing them in the name of the Father, and of the Son, and of the Holy Ghost: teaching them to observe all things whatsoever I have commanded you: and, lo, I am with you alway, even unto the end of the world. Amen.
—Matthew 28:18–20

The change from the Man of Sorrows (Isaiah 53:3) before the Crucifixion to the *"Lord of all"* (Acts 10:36) after the Resurrection is very striking. Before His suffering, crucifixion, and death, Jesus was well-known by His disciples and appeared only in one form, as the Son of Man. He was dressed in the common, one-piece, peasant's garment of His day. As the Scriptures say, it was *"without seam, woven from the top throughout"* (John 19:23). However, after He had risen from the dead, there were several occasions on which He was not recognized by those who loved Him best, and He is at least once described as having appeared to two of them *"in another form"* (Mark 16:12). He was the same person, for they saw His hands and His feet, and Thomas even examined Him and placed his finger in the nailprints of His hands (John

20:26–29). Yet, it appears that some gleams of His glory were sometimes manifested to them, a glory that had been hidden during His previous life, except when He stood on the Mount of Transfiguration.

Before His death, His appearances were to the general public: He stood in the midst of scribes and Pharisees and publicans and sinners, and preached the Good News. But after His resurrection, He appeared only to His disciples, sometimes to one disciple at a time. Once He appeared to two of His followers, and on one occasion to about five hundred believers at once. However, He always appeared to His disciples, and to them only. Before His death, His preaching was full of parables; they were plain to those who had understanding, but they were often dark and mysterious even to His own followers, for it was a judgment from the Lord upon that evil generation that *"by hearing ye shall hear, and shall not understand; and seeing ye shall see, and shall not perceive"* (Matthew 13:14). But it is equally true that our Lord, before His death, brought His teaching down to the comprehension of the uninstructed minds that listened to it; He only slightly touched on many of the deeper truths because His hearers were not yet able to bear them (1 Corinthians 3:2).

Until His crucifixion, Christ veiled the splendor of many truths; after His resurrection, He no longer spoke in parables, but He brought His disciples into the inner circle of the great doctrines of the kingdom. He, as it were, showed Himself face-to-face to them. Before His death, the Lord Jesus was always with His followers, and they even knew the secret places where He went to rest and pray and be by Himself. But after He had risen, He came and went among them at irregular intervals for forty days.

For instance, once they were alone in a room with the doors shut, and suddenly He stood in the midst of them. Another time He called to them from the shore when they were fishing, and when they landed they found *"a fire of coals there, and fish laid thereon, and bread"* (John 21:9). He was seen in the garden on the Mount of Olives, He walked to Emmaus, He comforted the assembly at Jerusalem, and He showed Himself to the disciples at the Sea of Galilee. Yet where did He go when, after the various encounters, *"he vanished out of their sight"* (Luke 24:31)? Who can tell where He was during many of those forty days? Jesus' appearances were strange, and His disappearances were equally so. More-over, these examples show that, after He had risen from the dead, He had undergone some miraculous change, which revealed in Him what had been concealed before, although His identity was still indisputable.

It was no small honor to have seen our risen Lord while He still lingered here below. What must it be to see Jesus as He is now! He is the same Jesus as He was when He was here. In His real manhood, He sits glorified in heaven (Revelation 5:13) and is capable of being seen by the eye and heard by the ear. Yet how different He is. If we had seen Him in His agony, we would all the more admire His glory.

Let your heart frequently dwell upon Christ cruci-fied, but indulge yourself very often by thinking of Christ glorified. Delight to think that He is not here, for He is risen; He is not here, for He has ascended; He is not here, for He sits at the right hand of God and makes in-tercession for us. Let your soul frequently travel the blessed highway from the tomb to the throne. In Rome there was a *Via Sacra,* along which returning conquerors went from the gates of the city up to the heights of the capitol. Similarly, there is another "Via Sacra" that you ought to examine often, for along it the risen Savior went in glorious majesty from the tomb of Joseph of Arimathea to the eternal dignities of His Father's right hand. Your spirit will do well to see its dawn of hope in His death, and its full assurance of hope in His risen life.

In this chapter, I will endeavor to show, as God the Spirit helps me, both our Lord's resurrection power and the way our Lord exercises the spiritual part of that power in relation to us.

OUR LORD'S RESURRECTION POWER

"All power is given unto me in heaven and in earth." At the risk of repeating myself, I would like to begin by asking you to remember the Garden of Gethsemane and to bow your spirit in the shade of those gray olive trees at the sight of Jesus' bloody sweat. What a contrast between that scene and the time when Jesus made the statement in our text! The first scene shows the weakness of man, the bowing, the prostrating, the crushing of the manhood of the Mediator; but the second scene reveals the strength of the God-man. He is surrounded with omnipotence. Even though He was still on earth when He spoke these words, He had received the privilege, honor, glory, fullness, and power that lifted Him far above the sons of men. As Mediator, He was no longer a sufferer but a sovereign, no longer a victim but a victor, no longer a servant but the Monarch of earth and heaven.

Yet He never would have received such power if He had not endured such weakness. All power would never have been given to the Mediator if all comfort had not been taken away. He stooped to conquer. The way to His throne was downward. Mounting steps of ivory, Solomon ascended to his throne of gold, but our Lord and Master descended so that He might ascend. He went down into the awful depths of unutterable agony so that all power in heaven and earth might belong to Him as our Redeemer and Covenant Head.

All Power Whatsoever

Now think for a moment about the words, *"all power."* As a result of His death, Jesus Christ has been given all power by His Father. This is just another way of saying that the Mediator possesses omnipotence, for the word *omnipotence* comes from the Latin for "all power." What mind can conceive or what tongue can clearly explain the meaning of *"all power"*? We cannot grasp it. It is too high; we cannot reach it. Such knowledge is too wonderful for us.

The power of self-existence, the power of creation, the power of sustaining that which has been made, the power of making and destroying, the power of opening and shutting, of overthrowing and establishing, of killing and making alive, the power to pardon and to condemn, to give and to withhold, to decree and to fulfill, to be, in a word, *"head over all things to* [His] *church"* (Ephesians 1:22)—all this has been placed in the authority of Jesus Christ our Lord. We might as well attempt to describe infinity or map what is boundless than try to explain what *"all power"* means. Yet, whatever it is, it all has been given to our Lord; it all rests in those hands that once were fastened to the cross of shame. It all has been left with the heart that was pierced with the spear; it all has been placed as a wreath upon the head that was surrounded with a crown of thorns.

All Power in Heaven

"All power in heaven" is His. Take note of this! He therefore has the power of God, for God is in heaven, and the power of God emanates from that central throne. Jesus, then, has divine power. Whatever Jehovah can do, Jesus can do. If it were His will to speak another world into existence, we would see tonight a fresh star adorning the brow of night. If it were His will to immediately fold up creation like a worn-out garment (Hebrews 1:10–12), the elements would pass away (2 Peter 3:10) and the heavens would be shriveled like a scroll (Isaiah 34:4). The power that *"bind*[s] *the sweet influences of Pleiades, or loose*[s] *the bands of Orion"* (Job 38:31) is with the Nazarene; the Crucified One *"guide*[s] *Arcturus with his sons"* (v. 32). Angelic hosts are waiting in midair to obey the commands of Jesus of Nazareth (Psalm 103:20), and the cherubim and the four living creatures before the throne (Revelation 5:11–12) unceasingly obey Him. He who was *"despised and rejected of men"* (Isaiah 53:3) now commands the homage of all heaven, as the One *"who is over all, God blessed for ever"* (Romans 9:5).

"All power in heaven" relates to the providential skill and might with which God rules everything in the universe. He holds the reins of all created forces and impels or restrains them at His will—giving force to law and giving life to all existence. The old pagans dreamed of the god Apollo driving the chariot of the sun and guiding its fiery steeds in their daily course, but it is not so. Jesus is Lord of all. He harnesses the winds to His chariot and thrusts a bit into the mouth of the tempest, doing as He wills among the armies of heaven and the inhabitants of this lower world. The power that sustains and governs this globe emanates from Him in heaven, for

88

the Father has committed all things into His hands. *"By him all things consist"* (Colossians 1:17).

All the Power of the Holy Spirit

"All power" must include—and this has practical application for us—all the power of the Holy Spirit. In the work that lies nearest to our hearts, the Holy Spirit is the great force. It is He who convicts men of sin and leads them to the Savior, who gives them new hearts and right spirits, plants them in the church, and then causes them to grow and become fruitful.

The power of the Holy Spirit goes forth among the sons of men according to the will of our Lord. As the anointing oil that was poured upon Aaron's head ran down his beard and went down to the hem of his garments (Psalm 133:2), the Spirit that has been granted to Jesus without measure (John 3:34) flows from Him to us. Jesus has the *"residue* [remnant] *of the spirit"* (Malachi 2:15), and according to His will, the Holy Spirit goes forth into the church and from the church into the world, to accomplish the purposes of saving grace. It is not possible that the church should fail because of a lack of spiritual gifts or influence while her heavenly Bridegroom has such overflowing stores of both. All the power of the Holy Trinity—Father, Son, and Spirit—is at the command of Jesus, who is exalted *"far above all principality, and power, and might, and dominion, and every name that is named, not only in this world, but also in that which is to come"* (Ephesians 1:21).

All Power on Earth

Our Lord also claimed that *"all power"* had been given to Him on earth. This is more than could be truly said by any mere man; no mortal may claim all power in heaven, and when he aspires to all power on earth, it is but a dream. Men have strained to become king over the whole world, but they have seldom, if ever, attained this. When it has seemed to be within the clutches of their ambition, it has melted away like a snowflake in the sun.

Indeed, even if a man could rule over all his fellow-men, he still would not have all power on earth, for there are other forces that would scorn his control. Deadly diseases laugh at the power of men. When Naaman came to the king of Israel to be cured of his leprosy, the king cried, *"Am I God, to kill and to make alive, that this man doth send unto me to recover a man of his leprosy?"* (2 Kings 5:7). The king did not have all power. Wind and waves, moreover, scorn mortal rule. It is not true that even the British Empire ruled the waves.

By sickness and pain and death, the proudest princes have been forced to recognize that, after all, they were only men. Often, their weaknesses have been such that they have made it even more apparent that power belongs to God, and to God alone, so that when He entrusts a little of it to the sons of men, it is so little that they are fools if they boast about it. See, then, this wonder that is before us: a Man who has power over all things on earth without exception, and who is obeyed by all creatures, great and small, because the Lord Jehovah has put all things under His feet.

All Power over the Minds of Men

For our purposes, it is very important for us to remember that our Lord has *"all power"* over the minds of men, both good and bad. He calls whomever He pleases into His fellowship, and they obey. Having called them,

He is able to sanctify them to the highest degree of holiness, working in them all the good pleasure of His will with power. Believers can be so influenced by our Lord, through the Holy Spirit, that they can be impelled to the most divine fervor and elevated to the most sublime frames of mind.

I often pray—and I do not doubt that you have prayed in this way, too—that God would raise up leaders in the church, believers full of faith and of the Holy Spirit, standard-bearers in the day of battle. There are few preachers of the Gospel who preach with any real power. Even the apostle Paul could say, "You do not have many you can call fathers in the faith" (1 Corinthians 4:15). More precious than the gold of Ophir (1 Chronicles 29:4) are those who stand out as pillars of the Lord's house, strongholds of the truth, champions in the camp of Israel. How few apostolic men we have! We need Luthers, Calvins, Bunyans, and Whitefields again, men who are fit to make their mark on an era, whose names breathe terror in our enemies' ears. We are in dire need of such men. Where are they? From where will they come to us? We cannot tell in what farmhouse or business or school such believers may be, but our Lord has them in store. They are the gifts of Jesus Christ to the church, and they will come in due time. Let us believe in the power of Jesus to give us valiant followers of Christ and *"men of renown"* (Numbers 16:2). Who knows how soon He will supply them?

All Power for Our High Calling

Since *"all power...in earth"* has been placed in Christ's hands, He can also clothe any and all of His servants with a sacred might by which they will be equipped

91

for their high calling. Without bringing them out into the front ranks, He can cause them to occupy their appointed stations until He comes, fortified with a power that will make them useful. My brother, the Lord Jesus can make you extremely prosperous in the sphere in which He has placed you. My sister, through your influence and care, your Lord can bless the little children who gather at your knee. Perhaps you are very weak, and you know it, but there is no reason why you should not be strong in Him. If you are looking to those who are strong for strength, He can endow you *"with power from on high"* (Luke 24:49) and say to you as He did to Gideon, *"Go in this thy might"* (Judges 6:14). Your slowness of speech need not disqualify you, for He will be with your mouth as He was with Moses' (Exodus 4:12). Your lack of culture need not hinder you, for Shamgar struck down and killed the Philistines with merely an ox goad (Judges 3:31), and Amos, the prophet, was a herdsman (Amos 1:1).

Like the apostle Paul, your personal presence may be despised as being weak and your speech as being contemptible. However, like him, you may learn to glory in infirmity, because the power of God rests upon you (2 Corinthians 12:9). You are not hindered in the Lord but in yourself, if you are hindered at all. You may be as dry as Aaron's rod, but He can make you bud and blossom and bring forth fruit (Numbers 17:5–8). You may be nearly as empty as the widow's jar of oil (1 Kings 17:8–12), yet He will still cause you to overflow toward His people. You may think that you are as close to sinking as Peter was amid the waves, yet Christ will keep you from your fears. You may be as unsuccessful as the disciples who had toiled all night and not caught a single fish, yet He can fill your boat until it can hold no more. No one knows what the Lord can make of a man or what He may do through him. We are only certain of this: that *"all power"* is with Him by whom we were redeemed and to whom we belong.

Oh, believers, turn to your Lord in order to receive from His fullness *"grace for grace"* (John 1:16). Because of His power, we believe that if Jesus willed, He could stir the whole church at once to the utmost energy. Is the church asleep? His voice can awaken her. Does she inhibit prayer? His grace can stimulate her to devotion. Has she grown unbelieving? He can restore her former faith. Does she "[turn] *back in the day of battle"* (Psalm 78:9), troubled with skepticism and doubt? He can restore her unwavering confidence in the Gospel and make her valiant until all her sons are heroes of faith and put to flight *"the armies of the aliens"* (Hebrews 11:34).

Let us believe, and we will see the glory of God. Let us believe, I say, and once again our conquering days will come, when one will chase a thousand, and two will put ten thousand to flight (Deuteronomy 32:30). Never despair for the church. Be concerned about her, and turn your concern into prayer, but always be hopeful, for her Redeemer is mighty and will *"stir up* [His] *strength, and come and save* [her]*"* (Psalm 80:2). *"The LORD of hosts is with us; the God of Jacob is our refuge"* (Psalm 46:7). Degenerate as we are, One stands among us whom the world does not see, whose shoelaces we are not worthy to loosen. He will again baptize us with the Holy Spirit and with fire (Mark 1:7–8), for *"all power is given unto* [Him].*"*

All Power over All of Mankind

It is equally true that *"all power"* has been given to our Lord over all of mankind, even over that part of the

human race that rejects Him and continues in willful rebellion. He can use the ungodly for His purposes. We
have it on the inspired authority of the Bible that Herod
and Pilate, along with the Gentiles and the people of Israel, were gathered together to do whatever the Lord's
hand and will had determined beforehand would be done
(Acts 4:27–28). Their utmost wickedness only fulfilled
the unchangeable will of God. Therefore, He causes the
wrath of man to praise Him (Psalm 76:10) and the most
rebellious wills to be subservient to His sacred purposes.
Jesus' kingdom rules over all.

The powers of hell and all their armies, along with
the kings of the earth and the rulers, set themselves
against God and take counsel together (Psalm 2:2); yet,
the whole time, their rage is working out His purposes.
Little do they know that they are just slaves of the King
of Kings, dishwashers in the kitchen of His imperial pal-
ace. All things act as He commands. His will is not
thwarted; His resolves are not defeated. The pleasure of
the Lord prospers in His hands.

By faith, I see Him ruling and overruling on land
and sea, and in all deep places—guiding the decisions of
parliaments, dictating to dictators, commanding princes,
and ruling emperors. If He merely arises, those who hate
Him will flee from Him. As smoke is waved away, He will
drive them away. As wax melts before a fire, all His
enemies will perish at His presence.

Regarding sinful men in general, the Redeemer has
power over their minds in a way that is marvelous to
contemplate. In the history of the Old Testament, the
people of Israel were always breaking away from God
and running after their idols. The Israelites were cured
of their sin for a little while, as long as some great
teacher or judge had power among them, but at his death

they turned aside to worship the queen of heaven or the calves of Bethel, or some other visible symbols. It is the same way today. Men are running after idols. Well, what next? Are we going to despair? God forbid that we should ever despair while all power is in the hands of Jesus.

A great philosopher has told us that it is absurd to suppose that prayer can have any effect on the events of life. However, if God were to inflict my nation with some judgment that is severely felt by all, this philosopher would become as quiet as a mouse. The direction of men's thoughts can easily be turned by our Lord. He can manage it as easily as a potter controls his potter's wheel. The times are safe in our Redeemer's management. He is mightier than the Devil, the heathen, and the ritualist, all put together. Let us give all glory to Him who has all power in earth and heaven.

All Power to Draw People to the Gospel

Our Lord also has the power to give, and He does give, people an inclination to hear the Gospel. A preacher should never be afraid of getting in front of a congregation when the Gospel is his theme. Jesus, who gives him a consecrated tongue, will provide willing ears that will listen to him. At His command, deserted sanctuaries grow crowded, and the people throng to hear the joyful sound. Yes, and He can do more than that, for He can make the word powerful so that thousands are converted. He can compel the frivolous to think, the obstinately heretical to accept the truth, and those who are hardened to yield to His gracious rule.

He has the key to every human heart. *"He...openeth, and no man shutteth; and shutteth, and no man openeth"* (Revelation 3:7). He will clothe His Word with power and will subdue the nations by it. It is our job to proclaim the Gospel and to believe that no one is beyond the saving power of Jesus Christ. Although he may have been dyed many times in the scarlet dye of depravity, the sinner may be cleansed and the ringleader of immorality may become a pattern of holiness. The Pharisee can be converted—think of the apostle Paul. Even priests may be saved, for did not a great multitude of the priests believe? There is no one in any conceivable condition of sin who is beyond the power of Christ. He may have gone to the uttermost in sin, so that he stands on the verge of hell, but if Jesus stretches out His pierced hand, he will be pulled out like a brand from the fire (Zechariah 3:2).

Beloved, I have no doubts, I entertain no fears, for every moment of time is bringing closer the magnificent display of the power of Jesus. You may despise the Gospel you have heard preached. Christ may have been presented to you, and you may have rejected Him. But God will change the way He deals with you before long, and your contempt and rejection will then come to an end, for the same Jesus who ascended into heaven from the Mount of Olives will return in the manner that He was seen going up into heaven. He will descend with matchless ceremony and power, and this astonished world that saw Him crucified will see Him enthroned. In the same place where men dogged His heels and persecuted Him, they will crowd around Him to pay Him homage, for He will reign and will put His enemies under His feet. This same earth that once was troubled with His griefs will rejoice in His triumphs.

All Power to Raise Us from the Dead

And there is more. You may be dead before the Lord comes, but you will know that *"all power"* is His, for at the blast of His trumpet, your body will rise again to stand before His fearful judgment seat. You may have resisted Him here, but you will be unable to oppose Him then; you may despise Him now, but then you will have to tremble before Him. Jesus' statement, *"Depart from me, ye cursed"* (Matthew 25:41), will prove to you in a frightful way that He has *"all power,"* if you will not now accept it by coming to Him who invites the weary and the heavily burdened to come to Him and receive His rest (Matthew 11:28). *"Kiss the Son, lest he be angry, and ye perish from the way, when his wrath is kindled but a little. Blessed are all they that put their trust in him"* (Psalm 2:12).

OUR LORD'S WAY OF EXERCISING HIS POWER

Secondly, I want to show you the usual way in which our Lord exercises His great spiritual power. Beloved, the Lord Jesus might have said, "All power has been given to Me in heaven and earth; therefore, take your swords and kill all My enemies who crucified Me." But He had no thoughts of revenge. He might have said, "These Jews put Me to death, and they will never receive My grace; therefore, go right away to Tarshish and preach." But no, He said to begin at Jerusalem (Acts 1:8) and He commanded His disciples to first preach the Gospel to His murderers.

As a result of the fact that Jesus has *"all power,"* His servants were commanded to disciple all nations. My brothers and sisters, the method by which Jesus proposes to *"subdue all things unto himself"* (Philippians 3:21) appears to be utterly inadequate. He wants His followers to teach, to make disciples, to baptize these disciples, and to instruct them further in the faith! Good

Master, are these the weapons of our warfare? Are these Your weapons of war? The rulers of this world do not contemplate conquest in this way, for they rely on huge guns, battleships, and weapons of deadly power. Yet, what are these but proofs of their weakness? If they had all power in themselves, they would not need such instruments. Only He who has all power can fulfill His commands with a word and dispense with all force but that of love.

Note that teaching and preaching are the Lord's way of displaying His power. Today we are told that the way to save souls is to decorate an altar with different colored silks and satins, variable according to the seasons, and to array priests in garments of various colors. With these ribbons and embroideries, joined with the burning of incense, genuflecting, and rituals, souls are supposed to be saved. Yet the Master said, *"Go ye into all the world, and preach the gospel to every creature"* (Mark 16:15). Preaching and teaching and baptizing the disciples are Christ's way. If Christ had ordained that we should be saved through observing the sacraments, they would succeed in this purpose, but He has ordained nothing of the kind. His mandate is this: "All power has been given to Me in heaven and earth. Therefore, go and disciple and baptize, and then still further instruct in the name of the triune God."

My brothers and sisters, remember who the men were who were sent to proclaim the message of the Gospel. The eleven who were foremost were mostly fishermen. Did the omnipotent Jesus choose fishermen to subdue the world? He did, and He still chooses humble men and women, because He needs no help from them; all power is His. People say that we must have an educated ministry, and by an "educated" ministry, they do not mean the ministry of a man of common sense, clear head, warm heart, deep experience, and great familiarity with human nature. Instead, they mean the ministry of mere classical and empirical students, theorists, and novices who are more learned in modern infidelities than in the truth of God. If our Lord had wished to employ the worldly-wise, He certainly might have chosen eleven men from Corinth or from Athens who would have commanded popular respect for their accomplishments, or He could have found eleven learned rabbis nearer to home. However, He did not need such men. Their vain attainments were of no value in His eyes. He chose honest, hearty men who were childlike enough to learn the truth and bold enough to speak it when they knew it.

The church must get rid of her notion that she must depend on the learning of this world. I do not have a word to say against a sound education, especially an education in the Scriptures, but to replace the gift of the Holy Spirit with academic degrees, or to value the present style of so-called culture above our spiritual edification, is to set up an idol in the house of the living God. The Lord can use the most illiterate man as well as the most learned, if it so pleases Him. He said, "Go, you fishermen; go, and teach all nations." Carnal reason criticizes this as a weak method that is to be accomplished by even weaker instruments!

Now, let me state here that the work of preaching the Gospel, which is Christ's way of using His power among men, is based only upon that fact that He has that power. Some preachers say, "You must not preach the Gospel to a dead sinner, because the sinner has no power." It is true that the sinner has no spiritual life or power within him, but our reason for preaching to him is that all power has been given to Jesus, and He commands us to *preach the gospel to every creature*" (Mark 16:15).

I tell you this, if my Lord and Master should ask me to go tomorrow to the cemetery and command the dead to rise, I would do it with as much pleasure as I preach the Gospel to my congregation. I would do it for the same reason that leads me to urge the unregenerate to repent and be converted, for I regard such men as being dead in sin, and yet I tell them to live, because my Master commands me to do so. That I am right in doing this is proven by the fact that, while I am preaching, sinners do live. Blessed be His name, thousands of them have been quickened into life.

The prophet Ezekiel had to cry out, "You dry bones, live!" What a foolish thing to say! But God justified His servant in doing this, and an exceedingly great army stood upon their feet in what was once a large sepulcher. Joshua and the Israelites were commanded to march around Jericho while the priests blew trumpets; it was a most absurd thing to blow trumpets to cause city walls to fall down, but they came down, even so. Gideon's men were commanded simply to carry lamps within jars and to break their jars and stand still and cry aloud, *"The sword of the LORD, and of Gideon"* (Judges 7:18); it was a most ridiculous thing to hope to conquer the Midianites in this way, but they were conquered, for God never sends His servants on a fool's errand. It pleases God to accomplish His divine purpose by the foolishness of preaching—not because of the power of the preaching or the power of the preacher or any power in those who are preached to, but because *"all power...in heaven and in earth"* has been given to Christ and He chooses to work by the teaching of the Word.

Our business, then, is this: as our text says, we are to *"teach,"* which, in the original Greek, means "to make disciples." The business of each one of us, according to the grace we have been given (Ephesians 4:7), is to tell our fellowmen the Gospel and to try to teach them to become disciples of Jesus. When they become disciples, our next duty is to give them the sign of discipleship by *"baptizing them."* This symbolic burial testifies to their death in Jesus to their former selves and their resurrection to newness of life through Him. Baptism enrolls and seals disciples, and we must not omit or misuse this practice. When the disciple is enrolled, then the missionary or evangelist becomes a pastor, *"teaching them to observe all things whatsoever* [Jesus has] *commanded."*

The disciple is admitted into the school of faith by obeying the command regarding baptism; and then he goes on to learn, and as he learns, he teaches others also. He is taught obedience, not to some things, but to all things that Christ has commanded. He is not put into the church to become a legislator or one who devises new doctrines and ceremonies, but to believe what Christ tells him and to do what Christ commands him.

I want to end this particular chapter in a very practical way. Probably most of my readers are people who have believed in Jesus, who have been baptized, and who have been further instructed. You believe that Jesus has all power and that He works through the teaching and preaching of the Gospel, and therefore I wish to press a question home to you. How much are you doing toward teaching all nations? This charge has been committed to you as well as to me; for this purpose we are sent into the world. We have received so that we may distribute. How much have you distributed?

Dear brother, dear sister, to how many have you told the story of redemption by the blood of Jesus? Perhaps you have been a believer for some time now. To whom have you spoken about Jesus, or to whom have you written about Him? Are you distributing, as best you can, the words others have spoken or written about the Gospel, if you are not able to formulate the words yourself? Do not reply, "I belong to a church that is doing much for the Gospel." That is not the point. I am speaking of what you are doing personally. Jesus did not die for us by proxy, but He bore *our sins in his own body on the tree"* (1 Peter 2:24). I ask, then, what are you doing personally? Are you doing anything at all? I can imagine someone saying, "But I cannot become a missionary." Are you sure you cannot? I have been waiting for a time when numbers of Christians will feel that they must go to preach the Gospel overseas and will relinquish comforts and compensations for the Lord's sake. There can be no greater honor to a church than to have many sons and daughters bearing the brunt of the battle for the Lord.

Therefore, I want to place the Great Commission before you today like a battle standard. If God has touched your heart, rally to this call without delay. The heathen are perishing; they are dying without Christ by the millions, and Christ's last command to us was, *"Go ye therefore, and teach all nations."* Are you obeying it? I can hear someone saying, "I cannot go. I have a family and many ties that commit me to staying here." Then, I will ask you, my dear brother, are you going as far as you can? Do you travel to the utmost length of the providential rope that has tied you where you are? Can you say yes? Then what are you doing to help others to go overseas?

As I was thinking over this chapter, I reflected on how very little most of us are doing toward sending the Gospel abroad. Many churches are doing a fair share for unbelievers here at home, and I rejoice at the thought of it. Yet how much a year do we as individuals give to foreign missions? Write down how much you give per year for missions, and then calculate what percentage that is of your income. For example, "April: Gave to the missions collection x amount." Many of us give only a pittance every year toward the salvation of the world! Perhaps your financial record will read: "Income, $25,000. Annual contribution to missions, $5."

How does that look? I cannot read your heart, but I could read your checkbook and calculate a number in proportion. I suggest that you do it for yourself while I also take a look at my own expenditures. Let us see what more can be done to help spread the Redeemer's kingdom, for *"all power"* is with Him, and when His people are stirred up to believe in that power and to use the simple but potent machinery of the preaching of the Gospel to all nations, then *"God, even our own God, shall bless us. God shall bless us; and all the ends of the earth shall fear him"* (Psalm 67:6–7).

Chapter Six

Being Resurrected with Christ

But God, who is rich in mercy, for his great love
wherewith he loved us, even when we were dead in sins,
hath quickened us together with Christ,
(by grace ye are saved).
—Ephesians 2:4–5

These days, there are conferences featuring all sorts of people on all kinds of subjects, but it would be a remarkable thing if it were possible to have a conference of people who have been raised from the dead! If you could somehow or other get together the son of the Shunammite (2 Kings 4:25–37), the daughter of Jairus (Mark 5:35–42), the son of the widow at the gates of Nain (Luke 7:11–15), Lazarus (John 11:38–44), and Eutychus (Acts 20:9–12), what strange discussions they might have with one another! What extraordinary inquiries might they make, and what remarkable disclosures might they present to us! This, of course, is not possible, and yet a better and more remarkable group than this may easily be gathered on the same terms, and even more important information may be obtained from the disclosures of its members.

Indeed, there is a conference of that very nature among many of those who gather for church each week, for a great number of us were dead in trespasses and sins, but through God's power we have been quickened from that spiritual death and have been made alive to praise God. *"You hath he quickened, who were dead in trespasses and sins"* (Ephesians 2:1). As believers sit together in church, they make up an assembly of people who possess resurrection life, and they are a more notable assembly than they would be if only their bodies and not their spirits had been quickened.

Up until now, I have mainly discussed the events and implications of our Lord's own resurrection. Now I want to focus more specifically on how Christ's resurrection affects the lives of believers and how it gives us the hope of eternal life and of the resurrection of our own bodies.

To begin to understand what this means, we will need to review the past, rejoice in the present, and look forward to the future. Therefore, in this chapter, we will first discuss what it means for men to be spiritually dead. Then we will consider the miracle of new life in Christ, in which dead men are made alive. Next, we will observe the vital relationship that is indicated in the text. Lastly, we will conclude with a song, for the text reads somewhat like music—it is full of thankfulness, and thankfulness is the essence of true song. It is full of holy and adoring wonder; it is true poetry, even though it is expressed in prose.

MEN ARE SPIRITUALLY DEAD IN THEIR SINS

Let us first note a great and solemn truth by descending into the graveyard of our poor humanity. According to the teaching of sacred Scripture, men are dead, spiritually dead. Certain vain men would conclude that mankind is only a little disordered and bruised by the Fall, wounded in a few fragile parts of its body, but not mortally injured. However, the Word of God is very clear on the subject. It declares that the human race is not only wounded, not merely hurt, but has been killed outright and has been left for dead in trespasses and sin.

There are those who imagine that fallen human nature has only suffered a sort of blackout or fainting fit and just needs a process of reviving for it to be set right. They claim that you only have to get its blood circulating by education and by other manipulations, and to excite within it some degree of action, and then life will quickly be developed. There is much good in every man, and you only have to bring it out by training and example.

This fictional idea is exactly the opposite of the teaching of sacred Scripture. Within its truthful pages, we do not read of any fainting fit or temporary paralysis. Death is the name of the human condition, and quickening is what human nature desperately needs. Man is not partly dead, like a half-drowned sailor, so that some spark of life may yet remain if it is lovingly cared for and wisely nurtured. There is not a spark of spiritual life left in man—mankind is an absolute corpse to all spiritual things. God said to our first parents, *"Of the tree of the knowledge of good and evil, thou shalt not eat of it: for in the day that thou eatest thereof thou shalt surely die"* (Genesis 2:17). And they did die—they died a spiritual death. Moreover, all their descendants, by their fallen human nature, also lie in this spiritual death. It is not a feigned death, or a metaphorical one, but a real, absolute, spiritual death.

Yet, you may say, "Are men not alive?" Yes, they are, but not spiritually. There are different degrees of life. First there is the vegetable life, but the vegetable is a dead thing compared to the vitality of the animal. Above the purely animal life rises the mental life, a vastly superior life. The creature that is only an animal is dead to both the joys and the sorrows of mental life. Then, high above the mental, as much as the mental is above the animal, rises what Scripture calls the spiritual life—the life in Christ Jesus. All men have the mental life, to a greater or lesser degree. It is a good thing to cultivate it, to get as much of it as one can, to put it to the best uses and make it serve the highest ends.

Imagine a person who is in all respects like yourself, with this one difference: his soul has died within him so that he only possesses his animal faculties but has no intellectual faculties; so that he can breathe, walk, sleep, eat, drink, and make sounds, but all his mental power is gone. You would then speak of him as being entirely dead to mental pursuits. He might be a very vigorous and well-developed animal, but his manhood would be dead. It would be of no use explaining a proposition to him, working out a problem on the blackboard for his instruction, or offering him even the simplest schoolbook, for if he had no mind to receive, how could you impart any knowledge to him?

Now, spiritually, this is the condition of every unregenerate man. It is of no use whatever, apart from the Spirit of God, to hope to make him understand spiritual things, for *"they are spiritually discerned"* (1 Corinthians 2:14), as the apostle Paul wrote. The carnal mind cannot understand the things of God. Even the best trained mind has no glimmer of an inward sense of spiritual things; it stumbles over the outward sense and loses the real meaning, not from a lack of mental capacity, but from the absence of spiritual life.

Oh, sons of men, if you really want to know God, *"ye must be born again"* (John 3:7). *"Except a man be born again, he cannot see the kingdom of God"* (v. 3); he cannot understand it; he cannot know it. The carnal man cannot understand the things of God, which are eternal and invisible, anymore than an ox can understand astronomy or a fish can admire the classics. Poor humanity is dead, not in a moral sense or in a mental sense, but in a spiritual sense, and this is the way in which the Word of God very definitely describes it again and again.

Consider the many bodies that are sleeping in graveyards. They are quite unconscious, are they not? Whatever goes on around them neither brings them joy nor causes them grief. Friends they have left behind may water their graves with their tears, but no answering sighs come from the gloomy caverns of the tomb. Triumphant armies may march over the dead in their graves, but the dead do not shout with those who triumph.

It is the same way with men who are spiritually dead. They are unaffected by spiritual things. They can hear of a dying Savior, whose groans might move the very adamant and make the rocks dissolve, without being moved at all. Even the all-present Spirit is not discerned by them, and His power remains unrecognized. Angels, holy men, godly practices, devout aspirations—all these are above and beyond their world. The pangs of hell do not alarm them, and the joys of heaven do not entice them. They hear mentally, in a way, but their spiritual ears have been firmly stopped up, and they do not hear.

A man who is totally deaf is not startled by a thunderclap. If he is totally blind, he is not alarmed by lightning flashes; he does not fear the storm that he does not discern. It is the same way with you who are at ease in your sins. You cannot discern the danger of your sin. You do not perceive the terror that rises out of it, or else, let me tell you, there would be no sleep for your lustful eyes and no rest for your frivolous spirits. You would cry out in grief the very moment you received life, and you would not rest until you were delivered from the evils that now guarantee for you a sure damnation. Oh, if you were only alive, you would never be quiet until you were saved from the wrath to come. Man is unconscious of spiritual things and remains unmoved by them because, in a spiritual sense, he is dead.

Try asking a corpse to assist you in the most necessary humanitarian efforts. Suppose an epidemic breaks out. Ask the buried one to kneel with you and implore the power of heaven to stop the epidemic; or, if he prefers it, ask him to assist you in purifying the air and attending to sanitary arrangements. You ask in vain, for no matter how necessary or simple the act is, he cannot help you in it.

It is the same way regarding spiritual things for those who are not redeemed. The carnal man can put himself into the posture of prayer, but he cannot pray. He can open his mouth and make sweet earthly music, but he is an utter stranger to true praise. Even repentance, that soft and gentle grace that ought to be natural to the sinful, is quite beyond his reach. How will he be able to repent of a sin of which he cannot feel the weight? How can he pray for a blessing when he has no power to perceive its value? How can he praise a God in whom he feels no interest, and in whose existence he takes no delight? I tell you that the man is quite as incapable of responding to all spiritual things as the dead are incapable of performing the natural activities and duties of daily life.

Someone may say, "If this is so, then why do you tell spiritually dead people to repent and be converted?" Why do I speak to the spiritually dead in this way and tell them to perform actions that they cannot do? Because my Master tells me to, and as I obey my Master's command, a power goes forth with the word that is spoken, and the dead are startled in their sleep. They awaken through the quickening power of the Holy Spirit, and those who cannot naturally repent and believe, do repent, believe in Jesus, escape from their former sins, and live. Yet, believe me, it is no power of their own that startles them from their sleep of death, and no power of mine that captures their guilty, slumbering consciences. It is a divine power that God yokes with the Word that He has given forth, when it is fully and faithfully preached.

Therefore, I have practiced my daily calling of commanding dead men to live, because life comes at the divine command. But dead they are, most thoroughly so, and the longer we live, the more we feel that it is so. The more closely we review our own condition before conversion, and the more carefully we look into our own condition even now, the more fully we know that men are dead in sin and that life is a gift—a gift from heaven, a gift of undeserved love and sovereign grace—so that every one of the living must praise God and not themselves.

One of the saddest reflections about the death of human beings is what happens to their bodies. Death in itself, though a solemn matter, is not as dreadful as what comes as a result of it. Often, when that dear body has first been forsaken by the spirit, those who have lost the dear one have still been inclined to kiss that cold brow. The countenance of the deceased has often looked even more lovely than in life, and when friends have taken their last glimpse, they have seen nothing revolting, but much that is attractive. Our dead ones have smiled like sleeping angels, even when we were about to commit them to the grave.

However, we cannot shake off a wretched awareness of what is sure to be revealed before long. It is only a matter of time, and corruption must set in. So it is with us all. *"When lust hath conceived, it bringeth forth sin: and sin, when it is finished, bringeth forth death"* (James 1:15). I solemnly remind you, dear reader, that this will be your destiny forever and ever, unless God quickens you. Unless God causes you to live together with Christ, you will be dead in this world, perhaps corrupt in this world, but certainly so in the next world, where all the dreadful influences of sin will be developed and exposed to the very fullest, and you will be cast away from the presence of God and the glory of His power.

DEAD MEN ARE MADE ALIVE

Now let us move on to something more pleasant, and observe a miracle: dead men made alive. The great purpose of the Gospel of Christ is to create men anew in Christ Jesus. It aims at resurrection and accomplishes it. The Gospel did not come into this world merely to restrain the passions or to teach the principles of men, but to infuse a new life into people that they did not possess as fallen beings.

Recently, I saw something that seemed to me to be a perfect picture of those preachers whose sole aim is to improve the morals of their hearers, but who have not learned the necessity of spiritual regeneration. Not very far from the shore where I was standing, a dozen or more boats were dragging for two dead bodies. They were using their lines and grappling irons, and, with hard rowing and industrious sailing, they were doing their best, most commendably, to recover the lost ones from the pitiless sea. I do not know if they were successful, but if they were, what more could they do with these bodies except give them a decent burial? The process of education and everything else, apart from the Holy Spirit, is like dragging for dead men so that they may be laid out, side by side, and buried in an orderly and decent way— there is nothing more that man can do for man.

The Gospel of Jesus Christ has a far different and higher task. It does not deny the value of the moralist's efforts or decry the results of education, but it asks, "What more than this can you do?" and the response is, "Nothing." Then the Gospel tells these pallbearers to stand aside and make room for Jesus, at whose voice the dead arise.

The preacher of the Gospel cannot be satisfied with what is accomplished by drawing men out of the sea of outward sin. He longs to see lost lives restored; he desires that a new life be breathed into them—one that is superior to what they have possessed before. Go your way, education, and do your best; you are useful in your sphere. Go your way, teacher of morality, and do your best; you, too, are useful in your own way. But if it comes down to what man really needs for eternity, both of you, put together, are of little worth. The Gospel, and the Gospel alone, fulfills what men need.

Man must be regenerated, quickened, made new; he must have fresh breath from heaven breathed into him, or the work of saving him has not begun. The text tells us that God has done this for His people, for those who trust in Him. Let us observe the dry bones as they stir and stand before the Lord (Ezekiel 37:5–10). As we observe them, let us praise the Lord that, according to His great love toward us, He has quickened us together with Christ.

Jesus Rose for You

The Mystery of Quickening

In this idea of quickening, there is a mystery. What is that invisible something that quickens a person? Who can unveil the secret? Who can track life to its hidden fountain? Beloved, you are a living child of God; what made you live? You know that it was by the power of the Holy Spirit. You believe that your new life was planted in you by God. As our text says, "[God]...*quickened us together with Christ.*" You are a believer in the supernatural; you believe that God has visited you as He has not visited others and has breathed life into you. You believe correctly, but you cannot explain it. We do not understand the nature of wind, "*whence it cometh, and whither it goeth: so is every one that is born of the Spirit*" (John 3:8).

If someone purposely tried to sit down and attempt to explain regeneration, and the source of it, he might sit there until he turned into a marble statue before he would accomplish the task. The Holy Spirit enters into us, and we who had been dead to spiritual things begin to live by His power and indwelling. He is the great Worker, but how the Holy Spirit works is a secret that must be reserved for God Himself. We do not need to understand the method; it is enough for us if we share in the result.

The Reality of Quickening

It is a great mystery, then, but while it is a mystery, it is a great reality. We know and testify to the fact that we have been redeemed. And we have a right to be believed, for we trust that we have not forfeited our integrity. We know and testify that we now possess a life of

114

which we knew nothing some years ago; we know that we have come to exist in a new world and that the appearance of all things outside of us has totally changed from what it used to be. *"Old things are passed away; behold, all things are become new"* (2 Corinthians 5:17). I bear witness that today I am subject to sorrows that were not sorrows to me before I knew the Lord. I am also uplifted with joys that I would have laughed at the very thought of, if anyone had whispered them in my ears before the divine life had quickened me.

This is the witness of thousands of believers, and although others disbelieve us, they have no right to deny our experience simply because they have not experienced the same thing. If they have never tried it, what can they know about it?

Imagine that there were an assembly of blind men, and one of them had his eyes opened and began to talk about what he saw. Perhaps the rest of the blind ones would say, "What a fool that man is! There are no such things." One might declare, "I have lived in this world for seventy years, and I have never seen what he calls a color, and I do not believe in his absurd nonsense about scarlet and violet and black and white. It is all foolishness." Another man might declare, "I have been up and down and all over the world for forty years, and I declare that I never had the remotest conception of blue or green, nor had my father before me. He was a good soul and always stood up for the grand old darkness. He would say, 'Give me a good stick and a sensible Seeing Eye dog; I leave all your nonsensical notions about stars and suns and moons to fools who like them.'" In the same way that the blind man has not come into the world of light and color, the unregenerate man has not come into the spiritual world, and therefore neither of them is capable of judging correctly.

One day, at a public dinner, I sat opposite a gentleman who seemed to have a vast knowledge of wines and other alcoholic drinks, as well as all the tasty dishes of the table. He judged and criticized at such a rate that I thought he ought to have been employed by the caterer as the general taster. He had finely developed lips, and he smacked them frequently. His sense of taste was in a fine critical condition. He was also as proficient in the quantity that he consumed as in the quality, and he disposed of meats and drinks in a most wholesale manner. His retreating forehead, purple nose, and protruding lips made him, while eating, at least, more like an animal than a man. At last, hearing a little conversation around him on religious matters, he opened his small eyes and his great mouth and delivered this wise statement, "I have lived sixty years in this world, and I have never felt or believed in anything spiritual in all my life."

The speech was a needless diversion of his energies from the roast duck. We did not need him to tell us that. I, for one, was quite clear about it before he spoke. If the cat under the table had suddenly jumped on a chair and said the same thing, I would have attached as much validity to the utterance of the cat as I did to the declaration of this man. Until a man has received the divine life, his remarks regarding spiritual matters are of no consequence, even if he is an archbishop. He knows nothing about them, according to his own testimony.

When a person receives the divine life, he begins to exercise his renewed faculties. The man who begins to live for God now has powers that he never had before: the power to really pray; the power to wholeheartedly praise; the power to truly commune with God; the power to perceive God, to talk with God; the power to receive communication from the invisible world; and the power to send messages through the veil that hides the unseen (Hebrews 6:19), up to the very throne of God.

Suppose that a man has died and been buried, like others, in some great cemetery, some city of the dead, like the catacombs. Now suppose that an angel visits him, and by a touch of mercy, he lives. Can you imagine this man's first emotion when he begins to breathe? There he is in the coffin; he feels stifled, confined. He had been there for twenty years, but he had never felt inconvenienced until now. He had been comfortable enough in his narrow cell, if there can be comfort where there is no life. The moment he lives, he feels a horrible sense of suffocation. Life cannot stand to be so hideously compressed, and he begins to struggle for release. With all his might he lifts that dreadful coffin lid. What relief he experiences when the decaying plank yields to his pressure!

In the same way, an ungodly person is content enough in his sin, his covetousness, his worldliness. However, the moment God quickens him, his sin is to him as a sepulcher is to the living. He feels unutterably wretched in his condition. He is not at all in a pleasant place, and he struggles to escape. Often, with his first effort, the great black lid of blasphemy flies off, never to be replaced. Satan thought it was fastened down securely enough, and it was—for a dead man. However, life makes short work of it and throws off many other iniquities as well.

But let me return to my story about the man who was resurrected. He gasps for a minute and initially feels refreshed by the little air that the catacomb affords him. But soon he senses the clammy, damp air around him, and he feels faint and about to die. Similarly, the renewed man at first feels little except his inability, and he groans for power, crying out, "I want to repent. I want to believe in Jesus. I want to be saved!" Poor wretch! He never felt that way before. Of course he did not; he was dead, but now he is alive and he therefore longs for the evidences, signs, fruits, and refreshments of life. That frivolous nightclub was all right for one who knew no better; that bar stool was suitable for an unregenerate soul, but what can an heir of heaven do in such places?

The resurrected man cries out from the darkness of the tomb, "Lord, deliver me. Give me light and freedom. Bring my spirit out of prison so that I may live and praise Your name." He longs for liberty, and if, at last, he stumbles to the door of the vault and reaches the open air, he drinks deep breaths of the blessed oxygen. How glad he is to look upon the green fields and the fresh flowers! You cannot imagine that he would want to return to the vaults again. He will utterly forsake those gloomy places. He shudders at the remembrance of the past and would not for all the world undergo again what he has gone through. He is easily affected by every memory of the past and is especially fearful that there might be others who have been newly resurrected, like himself, and who may need a brother's hand to set them free. He loathes the place where he once slept so quietly.

The converted man also dreads the thought of going back to the joys that once fascinated him so completely. He says, "They are no longer joys for me. They were satisfactory joys for my old state of existence. However, since I have now entered into a new life, a new world, they bring me no more joy than the grave brings joy to a living man. I can only think of them with grief, and of my deliverance with gratitude."

Being Resurrected with Christ

WE ARE QUICKENED TOGETHER WITH CHRIST

Now, thirdly, the text indicates a vital relationship between the Redeemer and the redeemed: "[God] *hath quickened us together with Christ.*" What does that mean? It means that the life that lives in a saved man is the same life that dwells in Christ. Let me try to make this clear to you by an example from the Scriptures. We read that when Elisha had been buried for some years, a man who was dead was thrown into the tomb where the bones of Elisha were, and no sooner did the corpse touch the prophet's bones than it lived at once (2 Kings 13:21). It is the same way with the Cross of Christ. No sooner does a soul touch the crucified Savior than it lives at once, for the Father has granted Him to have life in Himself (John 5:26) and life to communicate to others (John 10:10). Whosoever trusts Christ has touched Him, and by touching Him he has received the power of eternal life. To trust in the Savior of the world is to be quickened through Him.

There are three senses in which we are quickened together with Christ.

Quickened through Christ's Representation

First, we are quickened through the representation of Christ. Christ represents us before the eternal throne. He is the Second Adam to His people. As long as the first Adam was spiritually alive, the race lived, and as long as the Second Adam lives, the race represented by Him lives before God. Christ is accepted, and so believers are accepted; Christ is justified, and so believers are justified; Christ lives, and so the redeemed enjoy a life that *"is hid with Christ in God"* (Colossians 3:3).

119

Quickened by Union with Christ

Next, we live by union with Christ. As long as the head is alive, the members of the body have life. Unless a member is severed from the head, maiming the body, it must live as long as there is life in the head. In the same way, as long as Jesus lives, everyone who is vitally united to Him, and who is a member of His body, lives according to our Lord's own word, *"Because I live, ye shall live also"* (John 14:19). Poor Martha was very surprised that Christ would raise her brother from the dead (John 11:21–25), but He said, as if to surprise her still more, *"Whosoever liveth and believeth in me shall never die. Believest thou this?"* (v. 26). This is one of the things we are to believe—that when we have received spiritual life, it is in union with the life of Christ; consequently, it can never die. Because Christ lives, our new life must remain in us forever.

Quickened in Christ's Likeness

We also live together with Christ in regard to His likeness. We are quickened with Christ in the same manner that He was. Christ's quickening occurred in this way: He was dead through the law, but the law no longer has dominion over Him now that He lives again. In the same way, you were cursed by the old Law of Sinai, but it has no power to curse you now, for you are risen in Christ. You are not under the law; you have nothing to do with its terrors and threats.

It is written of our Lord, *"In that he liveth, he liveth unto God"* (Romans 6:10). Christ's life is a life unto God. Yours is the same. From now on, you are not to live unto the flesh, you are not to *"mind the things of the flesh"*

(Romans 8:5). God, who gave you life, is to be the great purpose of your life; you are to live in Him and for Him.

It is also written, *"Christ being raised from the dead dieth no more; death hath no more dominion over him"* (Romans 6:9). The Christian lives in the same way. He will never go back to his spiritual death. Once he has received divine life, he will never lose it. God does not play fast and loose with His chosen; He does not save them today and damn them tomorrow. He does not quicken us with the inward life and then leave us to perish. Grace is a living, incorruptible seed, *"which liveth and abideth for ever"* (1 Peter 1:23). Jesus said, *"The water that I shall give him shall be in him a well of water springing up into everlasting life"* (John 4:14). Therefore, let us give glory to God. You who live by faith in Christ live an immortal life, a life dedicated to God, a life of deliverance from the bondage of the law. Rejoice in it, and give your God all the praise!

THE SONG IN THE TEXT

Lastly, there is a song in the text. I will write the score before your eyes and ask you to sing it at your convenience, *"making melody in your heart to the Lord"* (Ephesians 5:19). Brothers and sisters, if you truly have been made alive as others are not, you should, first of all, in the language of the text, praise the great love of God— great beyond all precedent. It was love that prompted God to breathe into Adam the breath of life and to cause poor clay to walk and speak. But now that the Fall has defiled us, it is far greater love that makes Him renew us with a second and yet higher life.

He could have made new creatures by the millions out of nothing. He only had to speak, and angels would have thronged the air. Or, beings like ourselves, only pure and unfallen, would have been multiplied by the tens of thousands upon the green grass. If He had left us to sink to hell, as the fallen angels have done before us, who could have opposed His justice? But His great love would not allow Him to leave His elect to perish. He loved His people, and therefore He would cause them to be born again. *"His great love wherewith he loved us"* defied death and hell and sin.

Dwell on this theme, you who have received His love! He loved us, we who are the most unworthy, who have no right to such love. There was nothing in us to love, and yet He loved us even when we were dead. In this wonderful truth, His great love seems to swell and rise to mountainous dimensions: love for wretched sinners, love for loathsome sinners, love for the dead and for the corrupt. Oh, heights and depths of sovereign grace, where are the notes that can sufficiently sound forth your praise? Sing, you redeemed ones, of His great love with which He loved us, even when we were dead in sins.

And do not cease to praise God as you think of the riches of His grace, for we are told that He *"is rich in mercy."* He is rich in mercy in regard to His nature, rich in the treasures of mercy in regard to His covenant, rich in the person of His dear Son through Christ's purchase of mercy, rich in providential mercy, but richest of all in the mercy that saves the soul. Friends, explore the mines of Jehovah's wealth, if you can. Take the key and open the granaries of your God, and see the stores of love that He has stockpiled for you.

Play your sweetest notes in praise of God *"who is rich in mercy, for his great love wherewith he loved us."* And let the last and the highest and the loudest note of your song be the same with which the text concludes:

"By grace ye are saved." Please do not ever hesitate about this. Brothers and sisters, whatever you do, whatever you believe about faith and works, never be slow to say, "If I am saved at all, I am saved by grace: grace in contrast to human merit, for I have no merit; grace in contrast to my own free will, for my own free will would have led me further and further from God. Protecting grace brought me near to Him."

Bless and praise the grace of God, and since you owe everything to it, exclaim, "May every thought of pride within me perish." Consecrate yourself entirely to the God to whom you owe everything. Desire to help spread the fragrance of that grace, which has brought such good things to you. And determine that He who has caused you to live by faith will, from this day until you enter into heaven, have the best of your thoughts and your words and your actions, for *"ye are not your own"* (1 Corinthians 6:19); you have been quickened from the dead, and you must live *"in newness of life"* (Romans 6:4).

The Lord bless you, dear friends. If you have never spiritually lived, may He give you grace to believe in Jesus today, and then you will be alive from the dead. And if you are already alive, may He quicken you even more by His eternal Spirit, until He brings you to the land of the living on the other side of the Jordan.

Chapter Seven

Following the Risen Lord

*If ye then be risen with Christ, seek those things which
are above, where Christ sitteth on the right hand of God.
Set your affection on things above,
not on things on the earth.*
—Colossians 3:1–2

L et me begin this chapter by reviewing some of the
essential truths of the Resurrection, so that we
may see how the Resurrection bears upon our
faith and service to Christ.

As we have seen, the resurrection of our divine Lord
from the dead is the cornerstone of Christian doctrine.
Perhaps I might more accurately call it the keystone of
the arch of Christianity, for if that fact could be disproved, the whole fabric of the Gospel would unravel.
*"And if Christ be not risen, then is our preaching vain,
and your faith is also vain...*[and] *ye are yet in your sins"*
(1 Corinthians 15:14, 17). If Christ has not risen, then
those who have fallen asleep in Christ have perished, and
we ourselves, in missing such a glorious hope as that of
resurrection, are of all men the most miserable (v. 19).

Because of the great importance of His resurrection,
our Lord was pleased to give many infallible proofs of it

by appearing again and again in the midst of His followers. It would be interesting to search out how many
times He appeared. I think that about sixteen manifesta-
tions are mentioned in the Bible. He showed Himself
openly before His disciples, and He ate and drank with
them. They touched His hands and His side, and they
heard His voice; they knew that this was the same Jesus
who was crucified. He was not content with giving evidence to the ears and to the eyes, but even to the sense of
touch He proved the reality of His resurrection.

As I wrote earlier, these appearances were varied.
Sometimes He met with one person alone, such as Peter
or Mary Magdalene. He conversed with two of His followers as they went to Emmaus, and with all the apostles by the sea. We find Him at one moment among the
eleven when the doors were shut because the disciples
were afraid of the Jews, and at another time in the midst
of an assembly of more than five hundred believers, most
of whom remained alive for years afterward and were
living witnesses to the fact. They could not all have been
deceived. As we have seen, it is not possible that any historical fact could have been placed on a better basis of
credibility than the resurrection of our Lord from the
dead. The fact of Christ's resurrection has been established beyond all dispute and question, and this was done
for a purpose, because it is essential to the Christian
faith.

This is also why the resurrection of Christ is com-
memorated frequently. There is no ordinance in Scripture that sets apart any one Lord's Day in the year to
commemorate the rising of Christ from the dead, for this
reason: every Lord's Day is the memorial of our Savior's
resurrection. Wake up on any Lord's Day you please,
whether in the depth of winter or in the warmth of
summer, and you may sing:

Today He rose and left the dead,
And Satan's empire fell;
Today the saints His triumph spread,
And all His wonders tell.

Therefore, setting apart an Easter Sunday to especially remember the Resurrection is a human practice,
for which there is no scriptural command. However, we
ought to make every Lord's Day an Easter Sunday to
honor Him who rose early on the first day of the week.
We gather together on the first rather than on the seventh day of the week because redemption is an even
greater work than Creation was, and is more worthy of
commemoration, and because the rest that followed
Creation has been far outdone by what follows the completion of redemption.

Like the apostles, we meet together on the first day
of the week, and we hope that Jesus may stand in our
midst and say, *"Peace be unto you"* (Luke 24:36). Our
Lord has lifted the Sabbath from the old and rusted
hinges on which the law had placed it long before, and
He has set it on the new golden hinges that His love has
fashioned. He has not placed our day of rest at the end of
a week of toil but at the beginning of the rest that remains for the people of God (Hebrews 4:9). On every first
day of the week, we should meditate on the resurrection
of our Lord and seek to enter into fellowship with Him in
His risen life.

WE ARE RISEN IN CHRIST

Let us never forget that all who are in Him rose
from the dead when He rose. Next in importance to the
fact of the Resurrection is the doctrine of the covenant

headship of Christ and the unity of all His people with Him. It is because we are in Christ that we share in everything that Christ did. We are circumcised with Him, crucified with Him, buried with Him, and risen with Him, because we cannot be separated from Him. We are members of His body, and not one of His bones can be broken. (See Psalm 34:20.) Because this union is most intimate, continuous, and indissoluble, all that concerns Him concerns us; therefore, since He rose, all His people have risen in Him. Moreover, we are risen in Christ in two ways.

Representatively

First, we are risen representatively. All the elect rose in Christ on the day when He left the tomb. He was justified, or declared to be clear of all liabilities on account of our sins, by being set free from the prison of the tomb. There was no reason for detaining Him in the sepulcher, for He had discharged the debts of His people by dying *"unto sin once"* (Romans 6:10). He was held hostage in our place and was our Representative, and when He came forth from His chains, we came forth in Him. We have endured the sentence of the law in our Substitute; we have lain in its prison and even died under its death warrant, and now we are no longer under its curse.

Now if we be dead with Christ, we believe that we shall also live with him: knowing that Christ being raised from the dead dieth no more; death hath no more dominion over him. For in that he died, he died unto sin once: but in that he liveth, he liveth unto God. *(Romans 6:8–10)*

Spiritually

Along with this representative resurrection is our spiritual resurrection, which is ours as soon as we are led by faith to believe in Jesus Christ. Then it may be said of us, *"And you hath he quickened, who were dead in trespasses and sins"* (Ephesians 2:1).

The full resurrection blessing is to be fulfilled later on at the appearing of our Lord and Savior, for then our bodies will rise again, if we fall asleep in Christ before His coming. If we are alive when He returns, we will be *"changed"* (1 Corinthians 15:51–52). Christ redeemed our humanity in its entirety—spirit, soul, and body—and He will not be content until the resurrection that has occurred in our spirits occurs in our bodies, too. These dry bones will live; as His dead body rose, our bodies will also rise.

> When He arose ascending high,
> He showed our feet the way;
> Up to the Lord our flesh shall fly
> At the great rising day.

Then we will know in the perfection of our resurrection beauty that we are indeed completely risen in Christ and that, *"as in Adam all die, even so in Christ shall all be made alive"* (1 Corinthians 15:22).

Now, for the purposes of this chapter, I want to discuss our fellowship with Christ only in regard to our spiritual resurrection. Do not misunderstand me, as if I think the Resurrection is only spiritual, for a literal rising from the dead is yet to come. However, our text speaks of spiritual resurrection, and I will therefore endeavor to explain what this means. Then I will discuss how we are to live the new life that we have received.

OUR SPIRITUAL RESURRECTION WITH CHRIST

Let us first consider our spiritual rising with Christ: *"If ye then be risen with Christ."* Though the words look like a supposition, they are not meant to be one. The apostle was not casting any doubt or raising any questions, but was merely putting it this way for argument's sake. It might just as well be read, "Since you then are risen in Christ." The *if* was used logically, not theologically; it was used for the sake of argument and not because of any doubt. All who believe in Christ are risen with Christ. Let us meditate on this truth.

Quickened by the Holy Spirit

We were *"dead in trespasses and sins"* (Ephesians 2:1), but having believed in Christ, we have been quickened by the Holy Spirit and are no longer dead. There we lay in the tomb, ready to decay. We lay in our death, quite unable to raise ourselves from it. Ours were eyes that could not see and ears that could not hear, hearts that could not love, and withered hands that could not be stretched out to touch Christ in faith. We were as guilty as if we had the power to do what is right, for the loss of moral power is not the loss of moral responsibility. We were, therefore, in a state of spiritual death of the most fearful kind. Then the Holy Spirit visited us and made us live.

Some of us remember the first sensation of life—how it seemed to tingle in our spirits' veins with sharp and bitter pain. We were like drowning persons who suffer great pain when life is coming back to them. We felt a dread of judgment to come and a sense of present condemnation. We were convicted of our sins, and we confessed our transgressions. However, these were signs of life, and that life gradually deepened and opened up until our eyes were opened. We could see Christ; our hands ceased to be withered, and we stretched them out and touched the hem of His garment. Our feet began to move in the pathway of obedience, and our hearts felt the sweet glow of love within. Then our eyes, not content with seeing, began to weep; and afterward, when the tears were wiped away, they glistened and sparkled with delight.

My brothers and sisters, believers in Jesus, you are not spiritually dead any longer. You have believed in Christ, and that great act proves that you are no longer dead. You have been quickened by God *"according to the working of his mighty power, which he wrought in Christ, when he raised him from the dead, and set him at his own right hand in the heavenly places"* (Ephesians 1:19–20). Now, beloved, you are new creatures, the offspring of a second birth, begotten again in Christ Jesus into *"newness of life"* (Romans 6:4). Christ is your life—a life such as you never knew before, nor could have known apart from Him. Since you have been risen with Christ, walk in newness of life while the world remains in death.

Changed in a Wonderful Way

Let us advance another step. We have risen with Christ, and therefore a wonderful change has been worked in us. The analogy of the seed is appropriate here. A buried seed rises from the ground, but not as a seed, for it puts forth a green leaf and bud and stem, and it gradually develops maturing flowers and fruit. In the same way, we wear a new form when we are resurrected in Christ, for we are renewed in the image of Him who created us in righteousness and holiness.

I ask you to consider the change that the Spirit of God has accomplished in the believer—a wonderful change, indeed! Before regeneration, the spirit was as the body will be when it dies; we read that *"it is sown in corruption"* (1 Corinthians 15:42). There was corruption in our spirits, and it was working irresistibly toward every evil and offensive thing. In many, the corruption did not appear on the surface, but it worked within. In others, it was conspicuous and dreadful to look upon.

Yet, how great is the change! For now the power of corruption within us has been broken; the new life has overcome it, for it is a living and incorruptible seed that *"liveth and abideth for ever"* (1 Peter 1:23). Corruption remains upon the old nature, but it cannot touch the new, which is our true and real self. Is it not a great thing to be purged of the filthiness that would have ultimately brought us down to hell, where the unquenchable fire burns and the undying worm feeds on the corrupt?

The apostle Paul told us that when a body is buried, *"it is sown in weakness"* (1 Corinthians 15:43). The poor dead frame cannot lay itself down in its last bed. Friendly hands must place it there. In the same way, when we were spiritually dead, we were utterly weak toward all that is good. When we were the captives of sin, we could do nothing good, even as our Lord said, *"Without me ye can do nothing"* (John 15:5). We were incapable of even a good thought apart from Him. However, *"when we were yet without strength, in due time Christ died for the ungodly"* (Romans 5:6), and now we know Him and the power of His resurrection. God has given us the spirit of power and of love. Is it not written, *"As many as received him, to them gave he power to become the sons of God, even to them that believe on his name"* (John 1:12)? This change from the natural to the spiritual is of such a nature that only God Himself could have done it, and yet we have experienced it. To God be the glory! Therefore, by virtue of our having risen in Christ, we have received life and have become the subjects of a wondrous change. *"Old things are passed away; behold, all things are become new"* (2 Corinthians 5:17).

As a result of our receiving this life and undergoing this change, the things of the world and sin become a tomb to us. Let me return briefly to the metaphor I used earlier. A sepulcher is as good a dwelling as a dead man can want. You may call it his bedroom, if you will, for he lies within it as unconscious as if he were sleeping. But the moment the dead man lives, he will not endure such a bedroom; he calls it a dreary vault, a loathsome dungeon, an unbearable tomb, and he must leave it at once.

In the same way, when you and I were natural men, and had no spiritual life, the things of this life contented us. A merely outward religion was all that we desired; a dead form suited a dead soul. Even in the early days of Christianity, Judaism continued to please those who were under its yoke. New moons and holy days and traditional ordinances and fasting and feasting were highly valued by those who forgot their resurrection with Christ (Colossians 2:16–17). All those things make pretty furniture for a dead man's chamber, but they are not appropriate for the living.

However, when eternal life enters the spirit, everything changes. These outward ordinances are flung off; the living man tears off his grave clothes, pulls away his shroud, and demands clothes that are suitable for life. Therefore, the apostle Paul told us to let no man take us captive by the traditions of men and the inventions of a dead ritualism (Colossians 2:8), for these things are not the portion of renewed and spiritual men.

In addition, all merely carnal things become as a grave to us, whether they are sinful pleasures or selfish gains. For a dead man, the shroud, the coffin, and the vault are suitable enough. But make the corpse alive again, and he cannot rest in the coffin; he makes desperate struggles to break out of it. By sheer force, he breaks off the lid, rips off his burial clothes, and leaps from the coffin. Similarly, the person who is renewed by grace cannot tolerate sin. It is like a coffin to him. He cannot bear evil pleasures; they are like a shroud to him; he cries for freedom.

When resurrection comes, the person lifts up the mound of dirt and grass above his grave and scatters both monument and headstone. Some souls are buried under a mass of self-righteousness, like wealthy men on whom shrines of marble have been heaped. However, the believer shakes all these off. He must put them away from himself; he cannot bear these dead works. He cannot live in any other way than by faith; all other life is death to him. He must get out of his former state. Again, a tomb is not a fit place for a living man, and when we are quickened by grace, the things of sin and self and carnal sense become dreary catacombs to us in which our souls feel buried and out of which we must arise. How can we who are raised out of the death of sin live any longer in it?

Wholly Raised from the Dead

Beloved, we are right now wholly raised from the dead, in a spiritual sense. Let us think of this, for our Lord did not have His head quickened while His feet remained in the sepulcher. He rose as a perfect and entire man, alive throughout His whole being. In the same way, we have been renewed in every way. We have received a perfect spiritual life, even though it is only in its infancy. We are perfect in Christ Jesus. In our inner man, our eyes have been opened, our ears have been awakened, our hands are active, our feet are nimble. All the faculties are there, though they are still immature and need development, and the old dead nature still has to be contended with.

Moreover, and best of all, we are raised in such a way that we will die no more. I no longer want to hear the dreary tale that a man who has received the divine life may still lose grace and perish. With our Bibles in our hands, we know better: *"Christ being raised from the dead dieth no more; death hath no more dominion over him"* (Romans 6:9). Therefore, he who has received Christ's life within him will never die. Has Christ not said, *"He that believeth in me, though he were dead, yet shall he live: and whosoever liveth and believeth in me shall never die"* (John 11:25–26)? This life that He has given us will be in us *"a well of water springing up into everlasting life"* (John 4:14). He Himself has said, *"I give unto [my children] eternal life; and they shall never perish, neither shall any man pluck them out of my hand"* (John 10:28).

On the day of our quickening, we say farewell to spiritual death and to the sepulcher in which we slept under sin's dominion. Farewell, you deadly love of sin; we are finished with you! Farewell, dead world, corrupt world; we are done with you! Christ has raised us. Christ has given us eternal life. We forsake forever the dreary habitations of death and we seek the heavenly places. Our Jesus lives, and because He lives, we will live also, world without end.

LIVING OUT THE NEW LIFE

Secondly, when we are resurrected with Christ, all of our attitudes and actions are to be transformed as well. We are urged by the apostle Paul to live out our resurrected life in suitable pursuits: *"If ye then be risen with Christ, seek those things which are above."* Our actions must be in agreement with our new life.

Leave the Sepulcher

If we are quickened, our first act should be to leave the region of death. Let us leave the vault of a merely outward religion, and let us worship God in spirit and in truth. Let us be done with rituals and all the dark business of religious exercises, and let the dead bury their dead (Matthew 8:22); we will have no part of it. Let us be done with outward forms and rites and ceremonies, which are not ordained by Christ, and let us know nothing except *"Christ crucified"* (1 Corinthians 1:23). Anything that is not of the living Lord is a mere piece of funeral array, fit for the cemeteries of formalists whose whole religion is like shoveling dirt on the lids of coffins. "Earth to earth, ashes to ashes, dust to dust." *"That which is born of the flesh is flesh"* (John 3:6).

Let us also abandon the vault of carnal enjoyments, in which men seek to satisfy themselves by making *"provision for the flesh"* (Romans 13:14). Let us not live by what we see or hear. Let us not live for the purpose of amassing wealth or gaining fame, for these ought to be dead things to the person who is risen in Christ. Let us not live for the world that we see or according to the ways of men to whom this life is everything. Let us live as those who have come out of the world and who, though they are in it, are no longer of it. Let us not think of the country out of which we came; let us leave it, as Abraham did, as though there were no such country. From this time on, let us dwell with our God as sojourners with Him, seeking *"a city which hath foundations, whose builder and maker is God"* (Hebrews 11:10). As Jesus Christ left behind the place of death, let us do the same.

And then, let us quickly forget every evil, even as our Lord swiftly left the tomb. After all, He stayed among the dead only for a little while. He had to lie in the heart of the earth for three days, but He made them as short as possible so that it is difficult to determine the three days at all. They were there, for we can identify fragments of each day, but surely never were three days as short as Jesus made them. He cut them short in righteousness, and, being released from the pains of death, He rose early, at the very break of day. At the first instant that it was possible for Him, consistent with the Scriptures, to get away from the sepulcher, He left the burial cloth and the grave clothes, and He stood in the garden, waiting to greet His disciples.

May it be the same way with us. There should be no lingering, no loitering, no yearning for the world, no clinging to its vanities, no making provision for the flesh. Get up early in the morning, you who are spiritually quickened! Get up early in the morning—from your ease, your carnal pleasure, your love of wealth and self—and get away from the dark tomb of spiritual death into a sphere of action that is compatible with your new life. *"If ye then be risen with Christ, seek those things which are above."*

To pursue the analogy, after our Lord had left the tomb early in the morning, He spent a period of time on earth among His disciples. In the same way, we are to spend the time of our sojourn here on earth in the same mind-set that Christ had, and in holy service. Our Lord considered Himself to be ascending from earth to heaven as soon as He rose. If you remember, He said, *"I ascend unto my Father, and your Father"* (John 20:17). He did not say, "I shall ascend," as though He looked at it as a future thing, but He said, *"I ascend,"* as if it were to happen so quickly that it was already an accomplished fact. Forty days He stayed, for He had forty days' work to do; but He looked upon Himself as if He were already going up into heaven. He was done with the world, He was done with the grave, and now He said, *"I ascend unto my Father, and your Father."*

In the same way, we have our "forty days" to sojourn here on earth; the period may be longer or shorter as the providence of God ordains, but it will soon be over. The time of our departure will come. Let us spend our risen life on earth as Jesus spent His—in a greater seclusion from the world and in greater nearness to heaven than ever. Our Lord greatly occupied Himself in demonstrating that He was indeed risen; He manifested Himself, as we have already seen, to His friends and followers. Let us also manifest the fruits of our risen life and bear testimony to the power of God.

Let all men see that you are risen. Live in such a way that there can be no more doubt about your spiritual resurrection than there was about Christ's literal resurrection. Let us spend the time of our sojourning here in the fear of God—worshipping Him, serving Him, glorifying Him, and endeavoring to set everything in order for the extension of our Master's kingdom, so that the redeemed are comforted and His sacred purposes are accomplished.

Ascend to Where Christ Is in Heaven

Now that I have led you up this far, I want to go further and rise higher. May the Lord help us as we seek to do so. Let our minds ascend to heaven in Christ. Even while our bodies are here on earth, we are to be drawn upward with Christ. We are to be attracted to Him so that we can say, "[He] *hath raised us up together, and made us sit together in heavenly places in Christ Jesus*" (Ephesians 2:6). Our text says, "*Seek those things which are above, where Christ sitteth on the right hand of God.*" What does this mean but rising to heavenly pursuits? Jesus has gone up; let us go up with Him. As for our bodies, they cannot yet ascend, for they are not fit to inherit the kingdom of God. However, let our thoughts and hearts mount up and build a happy rest on high. Do not let a stray thought ascend alone like one lone bird that sings and mounts the sky, but let your whole mind, soul, spirit, and heart arise, as when doves fly together as a flock.

Let us be practical, too, and truly seek the things that are above—seek them because we feel we need them, seek them because we greatly prize them, seek them because we hope to gain them—for a person will not wholeheartedly seek what he has no hope of obtaining. The *"things which are above"* that we are even now to seek are things such as the following.

Let us seek heavenly communion, for we are no longer numbered with the *"congregation of the dead"* (Proverbs 21:16), but we have fellowship in Christ's resurrection, and with all the risen ones. *"Truly our fellowship is with the Father, and with his Son Jesus Christ"* (1 John 1:3), and *"our conversation is in heaven"* (Philippians 3:20). Let us seek to walk with the living God and to know the fellowship of the Spirit.

Let us also seek heavenly graces, for *"every good gift and every perfect gift is from above"* (James 1:17). Let us seek more faith, more love, more patience, more zeal. Let us strive for greater charity, greater brotherly kindness, greater humility of spirit. Let us strive to be like Christ, *"that he might be the firstborn among many brethren"* (Romans 8:29). Seek to bear the image of the heavenly and to wear the jewels that adorn heavenly spirits.

"Seek those things which are above," that is, heavenly joys. I urge you to try to know, while you are on earth, the peace of heaven, the rest of heaven, the victory of heaven, the service of heaven, the communion of heaven, the holiness of heaven. You can have a foretaste of all these; seek them. In short, try to prepare for the heaven that Christ is preparing for you. You will soon dwell above; dress yourself for the great festival. Your treasure is above; let your heart be with it. All that you are to possess in eternity is above, where Christ is; therefore, rise and enjoy it. Let our hope anticipate the joys that are reserved for us, and in this way let us begin our heaven here below. *"If ye then be risen with Christ,"* live according to your risen nature, for *"your life is hid with Christ in God"* (Colossians 3:3).

The fact that Christ sits at God's right hand should be quite a magnet to draw us toward heaven. Where are the wife's thoughts when her husband is away but with the absent and beloved one? You know, my friend, it is not any different with us. The objects of our affection are always followed by our thoughts. Let Jesus, then, be as a great magnet, drawing our meditations and affections toward Himself.

Christ is sitting, because His work is completed, as it is written, *"This man, after he had offered one sacrifice for sins for ever, sat down on the right hand of God"*

(Hebrews 10:12). Therefore, let us rest with Him. Moreover, remember that He is sitting on a throne. Observe His majesty, delight in His power, and trust in His dominion. He is sitting at the right hand of God in the place of honor and favor. This is proof that we are beloved and favored by God, for our Representative has the choicest place at God's right hand. Let your heart ascend and enjoy that love and favor with Him.

Take wing, my thoughts, and fly away to Jesus. My soul, have you not often said, *"Woe is me, that I sojourn in Mesech, that I dwell in the tents of Kedar!"* (Psalm 120:5), and, *"Oh that I had wings like a dove! for then would I fly away, and be at rest"* (Psalm 55:6)? Now then, my soul, here are wings for you. Jesus draws you upward. You have a right to be where Jesus is, for you are married to Him; therefore, let your thoughts remain with Him, rest in Him, delight in Him, rejoice in Him, and yet again rejoice. The sacred ladder is before us; let us climb it until by faith we sit in the heavenlies with Him.

May the Spirit of God bless these words to you.

LIVING THE NEW LIFE

Now, inasmuch as we are risen with Christ, let us delight in purposes that are appropriate to our new life. This is where the second verse of our text comes in: *"Set your affection on things above, not on things on the earth."* The words *"set your affection"* do not quite express the meaning, though they come as close to it as any one clause could well come. We might translate it in this way: "Take delight in things above," or, "Industriously study things above," or, "Set your mind on things above, not on things on the earth." As we have seen, what is proper enough for a dead man is quite unsuitable for a risen one. Similarly, objects of desire that might have suited us when we were sinners are not legitimate or worthy objects for us once we are children of God. Since we have been quickened, we must exercise life, and since we have ascended, we must love higher things than those of earth.

What are these *"things above"* upon which we should set our affection? I ask you now to lift your eyes above the clouds and this lower firmament to the residence of God. What do you see there? First, there is God Himself. Make Him the subject of your thoughts, your desires, your emotions, your love. *"Delight thyself also in the LORD; and he shall give thee the desires of thine heart"* (Psalm 37:4). *"My soul, wait thou only upon God; for my expectation is from him"* (Psalm 62:5). Call Him *"God my exceeding joy"* (Psalm 43:4). Let nothing come between you and your heavenly Father. What does it mean to have all the world if you do not have God, and once you have God, what does it matter if the whole world is lost? God is all things, and when you can say "God is mine," you are richer than Solomon. Oh, to be able to say, *"Whom have I in heaven but thee? and there is none upon earth that I desire beside thee"* (Psalm 73:25). Oh, to be able to love God with all your heart and with all your soul and with all your mind and with all your strength! That is what the law required, and it is what the Gospel enables us to do.

What do I see next in the heavenly places? I see Jesus, who is God but yet is truly man. Do I need to implore you, beloved, to set your love upon the Well Beloved? Has He not won your heart, and does He not hold it now as under a mighty spell? I know you love Him. Then fix your mind on Him. Meditate often upon

142

His divine person, His perfect work, His glory as our Mediator, His second coming, His glorious reign, His love for you, your own security in Him, and your union with Him. Let these sweet thoughts possess your heart, fill your mouth, and influence your life. Let your morning begin with thoughts of Christ, and let your last thought at night be sweetened with His presence. Set your affection upon Him who has set His affection upon you.

But what else do I see above? I see the New Jerusalem, *"the city of the living God"* (Hebrews 12:22). I see the church of Christ triumphant, which is one with the church militant—that is, the church on earth. We do not often enough realize the fact that we have come *"to the general assembly and church of the firstborn"* (Hebrews 12:23), whose names are written in heaven. Love all believers, but do not forget the redeemed above. Have fellowship with them, for together we make one united communion of believers. Remember those

> Who once were mourning here below,
>   And wet their couch with tears,
> Who wrestled hard, as we do now,
>   With sins, and doubts, and fears.

Think about the brave ones who have won their crowns, the heroes who have fought a good fight and who now rest from their labors, waving their palm branches (Revelation 7:9). Let your heart often be with the perfected, with whom you are to spend eternity.

And what else is there above that our hearts should love but heaven itself? It is the place of holiness; let us love it so that we will begin to be holy here. It is the place of rest; let us delight in it so that by faith we may enter into that rest. Oh, my brothers and sisters in

Christ, you have vast estates that you have never seen. I think that if I had an estate on earth that was soon to be mine, I would want to take a peep over the hedge now and then and look at it. If I could not take possession, I would like to see what I had in trust. I would make an excuse to pass by it and say to any who were with me, "That estate is going to be mine before long." In your present poverty, console yourself with the many mansions you are to inherit. In your sickness, take great delight in the land where the inhabitants will no longer say, "I am sick." In the midst of your depression of spirit, comfort your heart with the prospect of complete happiness.

> No more fatigue, no more distress,
> Nor sin nor death shall reach the place;
> No groans to mingle with the songs
> Which warble from immortal tongues.

What! Are you chained to the earth? Can you not project yourself into the future? The stream of death is narrow. Can your imagination and your faith not leap over the brook to stand on the opposite shore for a while and cry, "All is mine, and mine forever. Where Jesus is, there I will be. Where Jesus sits, there I will rest, 'Far from a world of grief and sin / With God eternally shut in'"?

"Set your affection on things above." Oh, if only we could get away right now from these heavy cares that envelop us like a fog! Even we who are Christ's servants, and who live in His court, feel weary and droop at times, as if His service were hard. He never means for it to be a bondage, and it is our fault if we make it so. Martha owed service to her Lord, but she was not called to be

troubled over all her serving; that was her own doing. Let us serve abundantly, and yet sit, as Mary did, at the Master's feet.

You who are in business and who associate with the world by the necessity of your vocations, must find it difficult to keep well clear of the influences of this poor world that drag us down. The world will hamper you if it can. You are like a bird that is always in danger when it alights on the earth. There are snares and traps and nets and guns, and a poor bird is never safe except when flying at a great height. Yet birds must come down to feed, and they do well to gather their meals quickly and take to their wings again. When we come down among men, we must quickly go up again. When you have to mix with the world and see its sin and evil, be careful that you do not land on the ground without your Father. And then, as soon as you have picked up your seed, rise again and fly away, for this is not your rest. You are like Noah's dove, flying over the desolate waters; there is no rest for the soles of your feet but on the ark with Jesus. (See Genesis 8:9.)

Today, let us fence out the world. Let us chase away the raccoons and allow the vines to bloom and the tender grapes to give forth their good fragrance. Let the Beloved One come and walk in the garden of our souls, while we delight in Him and in His heavenly gifts. Let us not carry our burdens; let us consider today as a Sabbath unto the Lord. On the Sabbath, we are no more to work with our minds than with our hands. Cares and anxieties of an earthly kind defile the day of sacred rest. The essence of breaking the Sabbath lies in worry and murmuring and unbelief, with which too many are filled. Put these away, beloved, for we are risen with Christ, and it is not proper for us to be wandering among the tombs. Rather, let us sing to the Lord a new song and praise Him with our whole beings.

Chapter Eight

Will There Be a Future Bodily Resurrection?

Why should it be thought a thing incredible with you,
that God should raise the dead?
—Acts 26:8

We do not experience any distress concerning the spirits of our believing friends who have departed from this life. We feel sure that they are where Jesus is, and that they see His glory, according to our Lord's own memorable prayer in the seventeenth chapter of John: *"Father, I will that they also, whom thou hast given me, be with me where I am; that they may behold my glory, which thou hast given me"* (John 17:24). We know very little about the disembodied state; however, we know quite enough about the heavenly life of the redeemed to rest assured beyond all doubt that

> They are supremely blest,
>   Have done with sin, and care, and woe,
> And with their Savior rest.

Our main concern is about their bodies, which we have committed to the dark and lonesome grave. We

147

cannot reconcile ourselves to the fact that their dear faces are being stripped of all their beauty by the fingers of decay, and that all the marks of their humanity are fading into corruption. It seems hard that their hands and feet, and all the attractive framework of their noble forms, should be dissolved into dust and broken into utter ruin. We cannot stand at the grave without tears. Even the perfect Man could not restrain His weeping at Lazarus's tomb (John 11:35). It is a sorrowful thought that our friends are dead. We can never regard the grave with love; we cannot say that we take pleasure in the crypt and the vault. We still regret—and feel that it is natural to do so—that so dreadful a curse has fallen upon our race, that it should be *"appointed unto men once to die"* (Hebrews 9:27). God sent death as a penalty, and we cannot rejoice in it.

The glorious doctrine of the Resurrection is intended to take away this cause of sorrow. We do not need to be troubled about the body any more than we need to be troubled about the spirit. When we exercise our faith concerning eternal life, we are relieved of all our fears regarding the fate of the spirits of the redeemed. If we exercise the same faith concerning the Resurrection, we will with equal certainty remove all hopeless grief with regard to the body, for, although the body is apparently destroyed, it will live again—it has not gone into total annihilation. That very frame that we lay in the earth will sleep there for only a while, and, at the trumpet of the archangel, it will awaken in superior beauty, clothed with attributes that it did not have when it was on earth.

The Lord's love for His people is a love for their entire humanity. He did not choose them as disembodied spirits but as men and women arrayed in flesh and blood. The love of Jesus Christ toward His chosen is not an affection for their better nature only, but also for that which we are inclined to think of as their inferior part, for the Scriptures say, *"In* [His] *book all* [their] *members were written"* (Psalm 139:16), *"He keepeth all* [their] *bones"* (Psalm 34:20), and, *"The very hairs of* [their heads] *are all numbered"* (Matthew 10:30).

Did He not assume our entire humanity? He took a human spirit into union with His deity. However, He also assumed a human body, and in that fact He gave us evidence of His kinship with our entire humanity—with flesh and blood, as well as mind and spirit. Moreover, our Redeemer has perfectly ransomed both spirit and body. It was not partial redemption that our Kinsman effected for us. We know that our Redeemer lives, not only with respect to our spirits, but also with regard to our bodies, so that, even though the worm will devour skin and flesh, our bodies will yet rise again because He has redeemed them from the power of death and ransomed them from the prison of the grave.

It is a joy to think that, as Christ has redeemed and sanctified the entire man, and will be honored in the salvation of the entire man, our complete humanity will have the power to glorify Him. The hands with which we sinned will be lifted in eternal adoration. The eyes that have gazed on evil will see the King in His beauty. The mind that now loves the Lord will be perpetually knit to Him, and the spirit that contemplates Him will forever delight in Him and be in communion with Him. Yet, even more than all this, the very body that has been a clog and a hindrance to the spirit, that has been a chief rebel against the sovereignty of Christ, will give Him homage with voice and hand and brain and ear and eye. We look to the time of our resurrection for the accomplishment of our adoption, that is, the redemption of our bodies (Romans 8:23).

Now, even though this is our hope, even though we believe and rejoice in it to a degree, we nevertheless have to confess that questions sometimes suggest themselves to us, and the evil heart of unbelief cries, "Can this be true? Is it possible?" At such times, the question of our text is exceedingly necessary, *"Why should it be thought a thing incredible with you, that God should raise the dead?"*

Therefore, I will first ask you to look the difficulty in the face. Secondly, I will endeavor to remove the difficulty. There is only one way of doing so, and it is a very simple one. Then, thirdly, I will explore what the truth of the Resurrection means for us.

LOOK THE DIFFICULTY IN THE FACE

First, then, let us look this difficulty in the face. We will not for a moment flinch from the boldest and plainest assertion of our belief in the resurrection of believers, but we will let its difficulties appear on the surface. At different times, attempts have been made by misguided Christians to tone down or explain away the doctrine of the Resurrection and related truths, in order to make them more acceptable to skeptical or philosophical minds, but this has never succeeded. No one has ever been convinced of a truth by discovering that those who profess to believe it are half-ashamed of it and adopt a tone of apology. How can a person be convinced by someone who does not himself believe? For that, in plain English, is what it comes to. When we modify, qualify, and weaken our doctrinal statements, we make concessions that will never be reciprocated, and these concessions are only received as admissions that we do not believe what we assert. By this Samson-like cutting and trimming policy, we shear away the locks of our strength and break our own arms. That approach would never convince me, either now or anytime.

We do, then, truly believe that the very body that is put into the grave will rise again, and we mean this literally, just as we express it. We are not using the language of metaphor or talking about a myth. We believe that, in actual fact, the bodies of the dead will rise again from the tomb. We admit, and rejoice in the fact, that there will be a great change in the body of the righteous man, that its physical makeup will have lost all the mortality and tendency to corruption that now surrounds it, and that it will be adapted for higher purposes. For, whereas it is now only a tenement fit for the soul or the lower intellectual faculties, it will then be adapted for the spirit, the higher part of our nature. We rejoice in the fact that, although it will be sown in weakness, it will be raised in glory (1 Corinthians 15:43). Nevertheless, we know that it will be the same body. The same body that is put into the grave will rise again; there will be an absolute identity between the body in which we will die and the body in which we will rise again from the dust.

But remember that identity is not equivalent to absolute sameness of substance and a retention of the same atoms. I do not mention this qualification to take the edge off what I have just stated, but simply because it is true. We are conscious, as a matter of fact, that we are living in the same bodies that we possessed twenty years ago; yet, we are told, and we have no reason to doubt it, that perhaps not one single particle of the matter that constitutes our body now was in it twenty years ago. The changes our physical forms have undergone from infancy to adulthood are very great, yet we have the same bodies.

All I ask is that you acknowledge the same kind of identity in the Resurrection. The body in which we will die will be the same body in which we were born—everybody admits that, though it is certainly not the same in regard to all its particles. Indeed, every particle may have been exchanged, and yet it remains the same. Similarly, the body in which we will rise will be the same body in which we will die; it will be greatly changed, but those changes will not be such that they will affect its identity.

The Difficulty of Decay

Now, this hope is naturally surrounded with many difficulties, because, first of all, in the great majority of the dead, decay has taken place. The large majority of dead bodies have rotted and been utterly dissolved, and a large proportion of all other bodies will probably follow them. When we see bodies that have been petrified, or mummies that have been embalmed, we think that if all bodies were preserved in that way it would be easier to believe in their restoration to life. However, we may break open some ancient coffin and find nothing there but a little indistinguishable brown powder. We may open a grave in a churchyard and find only a few crumbled pieces of bone. Think of ancient battlefields where, even though thousands fell there, not a trace of man remains, since, as the years have gone by, the bones have completely disintegrated back into earth and in some cases have been sucked up by the roots and plants and have passed into other organisms. When we consider all this, it certainly does seem *"a thing incredible"* that the dead should be raised.

Our wonder increases when we remember in what strange places many of these bodies may now be. For the bodies of some have been left in deep mines where they will never be reached again; others have been carried by the ebb and flow of tides into deep caverns of the ancient sea. Some lie far away on the pathless desert where only the vulture's eye can see them or buried beneath mountains of fallen rock. In fact, is there anywhere that man's remains are not found? Who will point out a spot of earth where there is not the disintegrating dust of Adam's sons? Does a single summer wind blow down our streets without whirling along particles of what was once man? Is there a single wave that breaks upon any shore that does not hold some relic of what was once human? They lie beneath each tree, they enrich the fields, they pollute the brooks, they hide beneath the meadow grass. Yet, it is certain that from anywhere and everywhere the scattered bodies will return, like Israel from captivity. As certainly as God is God, our dead will live and stand upon their feet, an exceedingly great army (Ezekiel 37:10).

And, moreover, to make this miracle extraordinary beyond imagination, they will rise at the same time, or perhaps in two great divisions. The book of Revelation contains a passage that apparently teaches us that between the resurrection of the righteous and the resurrection of the wicked there will be an interval of a thousand years. Many think that the passage is referring to a spiritual resurrection, but I am unable to think so. The words must assuredly have a literal meaning. Read them, and judge for yourself:

But the rest of the dead lived not again until the thousand years were finished. This is the first resurrection. Blessed and holy is he that hath part in the first resurrection: on such the second death hath no power, but they shall be priests of God and

> *of Christ, and shall reign with him a thousand*
> *years.*   *(Revelation 20:5–6)*

Yet, granted that there may be this long interval, what a multitude will be seen when the righteous rise, *"a great multitude, which no man could number"* (Revelation 7:9). An inconceivable company that only God can count will suddenly leap up from "beds of dust and silent clay."

The break of a thousand years will be as nothing in the sight of God and will soon be over. Then the unrighteous will rise also. What teeming multitudes! Where will they stand? Which of earth's plains will hold them? Will they not cover all the solid earth, even to the mountaintops? Will they not need to use the sea itself as a level floor for God's great judgment? They will stand before God in an instant when the trumpet of the archangel rings out clearly and piercingly the summons for the Last Judgment!

And then, just imagine, the Resurrection in the case of the redeemed will not be a mere restoration of what was there before but will involve a remarkable improvement on anything we now observe. We put a bulb into the ground, and it rises as a golden lily; we drop a seed into the soil, and it comes forth as an exquisite flower, resplendent with brilliant colors. These are the same seeds that we put into the earth, the identical ones, but, oh, how different they become! In the same way, the bodies that are sown in burial are like many seeds, and they will spring up by divine power into outgrowths that will be more beautiful than anything we can imagine.

This increases the wonder of resurrection, for the Lord Jesus not only snatches the prey from between the teeth of the Destroyer, but what had become worm's meat—ashes, dust—He also raises in His own sacred image. It is as though a tattered and moth-eaten garment were torn to shreds and then by a divine word was restored to its wholeness, made whiter than any bleach on earth could make it, and adorned with costly fringes and embroideries that it did not have before—and all this accomplished in a moment of time. Let resurrection remain as a world of wonders, marvelous beyond all things. We will not, for a moment, attempt to explain it away or pare down the angles of its truth.

No Full Analogy in Nature for Resurrection

One of the difficulties of believing in the resurrection of the redeemed is this: there are positively no full analogies in nature that support it. There are phenomena around us that are somewhat like it, so that we can make comparisons, but I believe that there is no analogy in nature upon which it would be at all fair to found an argument. For instance, some have said that sleep is the analogy of death, and that our waking is a sort of resurrection. The metaphor is admirable, but it is very far from perfect, since in sleep there is yet life. A continuance of life is manifest to the person himself in his dreams, and also to all onlookers who choose to observe the sleeper, to hear him breathe or to watch his heart beat. But in death, the body has no pulse or other signs of life left in it; it does not even remain whole, as the body of the sleeper does. However, imagine that the sleeper is torn limb from limb, pounded in a mortar, and reduced to powder that is mixed with clay and soil, and then see him awaken when you call him—then you would have something worth calling an analogy! However, a mere sleep from which a man is startled, while it is an useful comparison, is far from being the counterpart of resurrection or an accurate picture of it.

More frequently, the development of insects is mentioned as a striking analogy. The *larva* is man in his present condition, the *chrysalis* is a type of man in his death, and the *imago* or perfect insect is the representation of man in his resurrection. An admirable metaphor, certainly, but no more than that, for there is life in the chrysalis; transformation is occurring. There is, in fact, the entire insect. No observer can mistake the chrysalis for a dead thing. Lift it up and look at it, and you will find everything in it that will eventually come out of it; the perfect creature is clearly dormant there. If you could crush the chrysalis, dry up all its lifeblood, beat it into dust, pass it through chemical processes, utterly dissolve it, and then afterward command it to become a butterfly again, you would see an analogy of the Resurrection; but this is unknown to nature as yet. I find no fault with using it as a comparison; it is most instructive and interesting. However, to argue that it is an example of actual resurrection would be childish to the last degree.

Nor is the analogy of the seed much more conclusive. The seed dies when it is put into the ground, and yet it rises again in due season. Accordingly, the apostle used it as the appropriate type and symbol of death. He told us that the seed *"is not quickened, except it die"* (1 Corinthians 15:36). What is death? Death is the resolution of an organism into its original particles, and so the seed begins to separate into its elements, to fall back from the organization of life into the inorganic state. But still a germ of life always remains, and the crumbling organization becomes its own food from which it builds itself up again.

Is this the case with dead bodies, of which not even a trace remains? Who can find the tiniest sign of life in a decayed corpse? I will admit that there may be some essential nucleus that those who are better instructed might perceive, but I would demand to know where in the corrupted body it is supposed to dwell. Is it in the brain? The brain is among the first things to disappear. The skull is empty and void. Is it in the heart? That also has a very brief duration, far briefer than the bones. Nowhere could a microscope discover any source of life in bodies exhumed from the grave. Dig up the soil in which the seed is buried, at anytime you desire, and you will find the seed where you placed it. However, this is not the case with a person who has been buried for a few hundred years. The last remnant of him has probably disintegrated beyond all recognition.

The generations that have not yet been born are not harder to find than those who have died. Think of those who were buried before the Flood, or who drowned in that global deluge. Where, I ask, do we have the smallest remnant of them? If you were to grind grains of wheat into fine flour, throw it to the winds, and then see wheat fields rising from it, you would have a perfect analogy. But as yet I do not think that nature contains a parallel example. The Resurrection stands alone. The Lord might well say concerning it, *"'Behold, I will do a new thing'* (Isaiah 43:19) in the earth." With the exception of the resurrection of our Lord, and the resurrection from the dead that was granted to a few people by miracles, we have nothing in history that is relevant to the point. Yet, we do not need to look there for evidence; we have far surer grounds to go on. Here, then, is the difficulty, and it is a notable one: *"Can these* [dry] *bones live?"* (Ezekiel 37:3). Is it a credible thing that the dead should be raised?

REMOVING THE DIFFICULTY

How are we to answer the problems that have been presented? I said that I would remove the difficulty. I did not make an empty boast; the matter is simple. We only have to read the text again with proper emphasis, and the difficulty will be removed. *"Why should it be thought a thing incredible with you, that God should raise the dead?"* It might seem unbelievable that the dead will be raised, but why should it seem incredible that God, the Almighty, the Infinite, will raise the dead? Grant that there is a God, and no difficulties remain. Grant that God exists and that He is omnipotent, grant that He has said the dead will be raised, and belief is no longer hard but inevitable. Impossibility and incredulity both vanish in the presence of God.

I believe this is the only way in which the difficulties of faith should be met. It is of no use to run to reason for weapons against unbelief. The Word of God is the true defense of faith. It is foolish to build with wood and hay when solid stones are available. My logic is, "God has said it," and this is my argument, too. If God declares that the dead will be raised, this is not incredible to me. The word *difficulty* is not in the dictionary of the Godhead. *"Is any thing too hard for the LORD?"* (Genesis 18:14). Heap up the difficulties, if you like; make the doctrine harder and harder for reason to comprehend. As long as it contains no self-evident contradiction and inconsistency, I rejoice in the opportunity to believe great things concerning a great God.

When Paul spoke our text, he was speaking to a Jewish ruler. He was addressing Agrippa, to whom he could say, *"King Agrippa, believest thou the prophets? I know that thou believest"* (Acts 26:27). It was, therefore, good reasoning to use with Agrippa to say, *"Why should it be thought a thing incredible with you, that God should raise the dead?"*

Will There Be a Future Bodily Resurrection?

First, as a Jew, Agrippa had the testimony of Job:

For I know that my redeemer liveth, and that he shall stand at the latter day upon the earth: and though after my skin worms destroy this body, yet in my flesh shall I see God: whom I shall see for myself, and mine eyes shall behold, and not another; though my reins be consumed within me.

(Job 19:25–27)

He had the testimony of David, who said, *"My flesh also shall rest in hope"* (Psalm 16:9). He had the testimony of Isaiah,

Thy dead men shall live, together with my dead body shall they arise. Awake and sing, ye that dwell in dust: for thy dew is as the dew of herbs, and the earth shall cast out the dead.

(Isaiah 26:19)

He had the testimony of Daniel, where the prophet said,

And many of them that sleep in the dust of the earth shall awake, some to everlasting life, and some to shame and everlasting contempt. And they that be wise shall shine as the brightness of the firmament; and they that turn many to righteousness as the stars for ever and ever. (Daniel 12:2–3)

And then again, in Hosea, Agrippa had another testimony in which the Lord declares,

I will ransom them from the power of the grave; I will redeem them from death: O death, I will be thy

plagues; O grave, I will be thy destruction: repen-
tance shall be hid from mine eyes.   *(Hosea 13:14)*

Therefore, God had plainly promised resurrection in the
Old Testament Scriptures, and that fact should have
been quite enough for Agrippa. If the Lord has said it, it
is no longer doubtful.

We Christians have been given even fuller evidence
of the truth of a future resurrection. Remember how our
Lord spoke concerning resurrection. With no restraint,
He declared His intention to raise the dead. This passage
in the book of John is remarkable:

> *Marvel not at this: for the hour is coming, in the*
> *which all that are in the graves shall hear his*
> *voice, and shall come forth; they that have done*
> *good, unto the resurrection of life; and they that*
> *have done evil, unto the resurrection of damnation.*
> *(John 5:28–29)*

This statement of Jesus is also extraordinary: *"And this*
is the will of him that sent me, that every one which seeth
the Son, and believeth on him, may have everlasting life:
and I will raise him up at the last day" (John 6:40).

The Holy Spirit has spoken the same truth by the
apostles. In that precious and blessed eighth chapter of
Romans, we have this testimony from the apostle Paul:

> *But if the Spirit of him that raised up Jesus from*
> *the dead dwell in you, he that raised up Christ*
> *from the dead shall also quicken your mortal bod-*
> *ies by his Spirit that dwelleth in you.*
> *(Romans 8:11)*

Will There Be a Future Bodily Resurrection?

Paul also wrote, *"But I would not have you to be ignorant, brethren, concerning them which are asleep, that ye sorrow not, even as others which have no hope"* (1 Thessalonians 4:13), and, "[Christ] *shall change our vile body, that it may be fashioned like unto his glorious body, according to the working whereby he is able even to subdue all things unto himself"* (Philippians 3:21).

I hardly need to remind you of 1 Corinthians 15, that great chapter with its massive argument for the Resurrection. Beyond all doubt, the testimony of the Holy Spirit is that the dead will rise, and since there is an almighty God, we find no difficulty in accepting the doctrine of the Resurrection and maintaining the blessed hope of the resurrection of the dead.

At the same time, it might be good to look around us and note what things the Lord has appointed to help us in our faith. I am quite certain, dear friends, that there are many wonders in the world that we would not have believed by mere report, if we had not come across them by experience and observation. The telegraph, even though it is an invention of man, would have been as hard to believe in a thousand years ago as the resurrection of the dead is now. Who in the days of pack horses would have believed in flashing a message from England to America? When missionaries in tropical countries have told the natives about the formation of ice—that people can walk across frozen water, that ships have been surrounded by mountains of ice in the open sea, and that the water has become solid and hard as a rock all around them—the natives have refused to believe such absurd reports. Everything is amazing until we are used to it, and resurrection seems incredible to us mainly because of the fact that we have never seen it; that is all. After the Resurrection, we will regard it as a divine display of power as familiar to us as creation and providence are now.

Will resurrection be a greater wonder than creation? You believe that God spoke the world out of nothing. He said, "Let it be," and the world came into being. To create out of nothing is quite as marvelous as calling together scattered particles and refashioning them into what they were before. Either work requires omnipotence, but if one had to choose between them, resurrection is the easier work of the two. If it did not happen so often, the birth of every child into the world would astound us. We would consider a birth to be, as indeed it is, a most transcendent manifestation of divine power. It is only because we know it and see it so often that we do not see the wonder-working hand of God in human births and in our continued existence. I repeat, the concept of resurrection only staggers us because we have not become familiar with it yet. There are other deeds of God that are quite as marvelous.

Remember, too, that there is one thing you have received on credible evidence, even though you have not seen it. It is the historical fact that Jesus Christ rose again from the dead. Jesus is the reason for your own future resurrection; He is the forerunner of it, the foretaste of it, the guarantee of it. As surely as He rose, you will rise. He proved that resurrection is possible by His own resurrection. Indeed, He proved that it is certain because He is the representative man, and, in rising, He rose for all who are represented by Him. *"As in Adam all die, even so in Christ shall all be made alive"* (1 Corinthians 15:22). The rising of our Lord from the tomb should forever sweep away every doubt regarding the rising of His people. *"For if the dead rise not, then is not Christ raised"* (v. 16), but because He lives, we will live also.

Will There Be a Future Bodily Resurrection?

Remember, my brothers and sisters, that as Christians you have already experienced within yourselves as great a work as the Resurrection, for you have risen from the dead in regard to your innermost nature. You were dead in trespasses and sins, and you have been quickened into newness of life (Ephesians 2:1). Of course, the unconverted will see nothing in this. The unregenerate man will even ask me what this means, and it cannot be an argument for him, for it is a matter of experience that one man cannot explain to his fellowmen. To know it, you must yourself be born again.

But, believers, you have already experienced a resurrection from the grave of sin and from the rottenness and corruption of evil passions and impure desires. God has worked this resurrection in you by a power equal to that *"which he wrought in Christ, when he raised him from the dead, and set him at his own right hand in the heavenly places"* (Ephesians 1:20). The quickening of your spiritual nature is a guaranteed proof to you that the Lord will also quicken your mortal bodies.

It comes down to this: our conviction of the certainty of the universal resurrection of believers rests upon faith in God and His Word. It is unnecessary to look elsewhere. If men will not believe the declaration of God, they must be left to give an account to Him for their unbelief. My friends, if you are God's elect, you will believe your God, for God gives faith to all His chosen. If you reject the divine testimony, you show that you are full of bitterness, and you will perish in it unless grace prevents it.

The Gospel and the doctrine of the Resurrection were opened up to men in all their glory to put a division between the precious and the vile. Jesus said, *"He that is of God heareth God's words"* (John 8:47). True faith is

the visible sign of election. He who believes in Christ
gives evidence of God's grace toward him, but he who
does not believe gives sure proof that he has not received
the grace of God. Jesus also said, *"But ye believe not, because ye are not of my sheep, as I said unto you. My sheep
hear my voice, and I know them, and they follow me"*
(John 10:26–27). Therefore, this truth and other Christian truths are to be held up, maintained, and delivered
fully to all of mankind to put a division between them, to
separate the Israelites from the Egyptians, the seed of
the woman from the seed of the Serpent (Genesis 3:15).
Those whom God has chosen are known by their belief in
what God has said, while those who remain unbelieving
perish in their sin, condemned by the truth that they
willfully reject.

WHAT RESURRECTION MEANS FOR US

Comfort in Bereavement

Now let us consider, lastly, what the truth of the
Resurrection means for us. Our first application is this:
"Children of God, *'comfort one another with these
words'*" (1 Thessalonians 4:18). Perhaps you have lost
those who are dear to you. Let me rephrase that; they
have passed into a better land, and the body that remains behind is not lost but has been invested in order to
gain blessed interest. You must grieve, but do not grieve
as those who are without hope (v. 13). I do not know why
we always sing mournful songs at the funerals of believers and why we drape ourselves in black. If I might have
my way, I would desire to be drawn to my grave by white
horses, or to be carried on the shoulders of men who
would express joy as well as sorrow in their attire, for

why should we grieve over those who have gone to glory and have inherited eternal life?

I like the old Puritan custom of carrying the coffin on the shoulders of believers and of singing a psalm as they walked to the grave. Why not? What is there, after all, to weep about concerning the glorified? Sound the joyful trumpet! Let the piercing tone of the trumpet sound forth the joyous note of victory! The conqueror has won the battle; the king has ascended to the throne of the great King. "Rejoice," say our fellow believers from above. "Rejoice with us, for we have entered into our rest." *"Blessed are the dead which die in the Lord from henceforth: Yea, saith the Spirit, that they may rest from their labours; and their works do follow them"* (Revelation 14:13). If you must keep up the signs of mourning—for this is natural—do not let your hearts be troubled. Praise God that, regarding those who have died in Christ, we may sing of His living promises.

Encouragement about Eternal Life

Let us, in the next place, be encouraged at the prospect of our own departures. We will soon pass away. Beloved, we too must die; there is no escape from this fact. There is an arrow, and there is an archer; the arrow is meant for my heart, and the archer will take deadly aim. There is a place where you will sleep, perhaps in a lonely grave in a foreign land, or perhaps in a mausoleum where your bones will lie side by side with those of your ancestors; but to the dust you must return. Well, let us not despair. It is only for a little while; it is only a resting place on the way to eternal life. Death is a passing event between this life and the next—let us meet it not only with composure, but with expectation, since it is not death now but resurrection to which we aspire.

Respect for Our Bodies

In addition, if we are we expecting a blessed resurrection, let us respect our bodies. Do not allow the members of your body to become instruments of evil; do not let them be defiled with sin. The Christian must not defile his body in any way whatsoever, either by gluttony or drunkenness or by acts of uncleanness, for our bodies are the temples of the Holy Spirit. *"If any man defile the temple of God, him shall God destroy"* (1 Corinthians 3:17). Be pure. When you were baptized, your bodies were washed with pure water to teach you that from that point on, you must be clean from all defilement. Renounce every evil thing. Bodies that are to dwell forever in heaven should not be subjected to pollution here below.

Lastly, and this is a very solemn thought, the ungodly are to rise again, but it will be to a resurrection of misery. Their bodies sinned, and their bodies will be punished. Christ said, *"Fear him which is able to destroy both soul and body in hell"* (Matthew 10:28). God will cast both spirit and body into a suffering that will cause perpetually enduring destruction to them; this is terrible, indeed. To sleep in the grave would be infinitely preferable to such a resurrection. The Scripture calls it *"the resurrection of damnation"* (John 5:29). The prophet Daniel referred to it as a rising *"to shame and everlasting contempt"* (Daniel 12:2). That is a dreadful resurrection. You should be glad to escape from it. Surely it would be dreadful enough for your spirit to suffer the wrath of God eternally, without your body having to be its companion, but that is the way it must be. If body and soul sin, body and soul must suffer—and suffer forever.

Will There Be a Future Bodily Resurrection?

English clergyman and author Jeremy Taylor told of a certain Acilius Aviola who was seized with a stroke. His friends thought he was dead, and they carried his body to the funeral pile to cremate him. However, when the heat had warmed his body, he awoke to find himself hopelessly encircled with funeral flames. In vain, He called for help. He could not be rescued but went from unconsciousness into intolerable torment. This will be the dreadful awakening of every sinful body when it is aroused from its slumber in the grave. The body will leap up to be judged, condemned, and driven from God's presence into everlasting punishment. May God grant that this may never be your case or mine, but may we believe in Christ Jesus now and so obtain a resurrection to life eternal.

Chapter Nine

The Power of Christ Revealed

For our conversation is in heaven; from whence also we look for the Saviour, the Lord Jesus Christ: who shall change our vile body, that it may be fashioned like unto his glorious body, according to the working whereby he is able even to subdue all things unto himself.
—Philippians 3:20–21

In this chapter, I am going to focus on the last part of the above Scripture passage, but I included both verses because they are necessary for its explanation. It would require several chapters to fully expound on a passage as rich as this.

Beloved, how intimately are our entire lives interwoven with the life of Christ! His first coming has meant salvation for us, and we are delivered from the wrath of God through Him. We live because He lives, and our lives are never more joyous than when we look very steadily to Him. Moreover, the completion of our salvation—the deliverance of our bodies from the bondage of corruption, the raising of our dust to a glorious immortality—is also wrapped up with the personal resurrection and quickening power of the Lord Jesus Christ.

As His first coming has been our salvation from sin, His second coming will be our salvation from the grave. He is in heaven, but, as the apostle Paul said in our text, *"We look for the Saviour, the Lord Jesus Christ: who shall change our vile body, that it may be fashioned like unto his glorious body."* We have nothing, we are nothing, apart from Him. The past, the present, and the future are only bright when He shines upon them. Every comfort, every hope, every joy that we possess, we have received and still retain because of our connection with Jesus Christ our Lord. Apart from Him, we are naked and poor and miserable (Revelation 3:17).

I desire to impress upon your mind, and especially upon my own, our need to remain in Him. In order to be zealous laborers for the glory of God, we must maintain daily communion with Jesus, for as it is with the blessings of His covenant, so is it with our *"work of faith, and labour of love"* (1 Thessalonians 1:3)—everything depends upon Him. All our fruit is found in Jesus. Remember His own words, *"Without me ye can do nothing"* (John 15:5). Our power to work comes wholly from His power. If we are to work effectively, it must always be according to the effectual working of His power in us and through us.

Let us first notice, from the text, the amazing transformation that will be accomplished by our Lord at His coming. Secondly, let us gain from it an understanding of the power that is right now proceeding from Him and is treasured up in Him. And thirdly, let us contemplate the work that we desire to see accomplished, which we believe will be achieved because of the power that is resident in our Lord.

AN AMAZING TRANSFORMATION

As we have seen, when Christ comes for the second time, He will *"change our vile body"* and make it like *"his glorious body."* What a marvelous change! How great the transformation will be! How high the body will ascend! Our bodies, in their present state, are described as *"vile"* in the King James Version, but the word in the original Greek is much more expressive, for it refers to our physical frame as "the body of our humiliation." Not, "this humble body"—that is hardly the meaning—but the body in which our humiliation is manifested and enclosed. The Lord will transform this body of our humiliation until it is like His own. And let us not just think of it as *"his glorious body,"* for that is not the most literal translation, but "the body of His glory," the body in which He enjoys and reveals His glory.

When our Savior was on earth, he had a body of humiliation (Philippians 2:8); that body was like ours in all respects except that it could not undergo decay (Psalm 16:10), for it was not defiled by sin. The body in which our Lord wept and sweat great drops of blood and yielded up His spirit, was the body of His humiliation. He rose again from the dead, and He rose in the same body that ascended into heaven. However, He concealed its glory to a very great extent, or else He would have been too bright to be seen by mortal eyes. Only when He ascended to heaven, and the cloud obscured the disciples' view of Him, did the full glory of His body shine forth to enrapture the eyes of angels and glorified spirits. Then His countenance became as the sun shining in all its strength (Revelation 1:16).

Now, beloved, we do not truly know what the body of Jesus is like in His glory. However, our present bodies, which are now in their humiliation, will be conformed to it. Jesus is the standard of man in glory. *"We shall be like him; for we shall see him as he is"* (1 John 3:2). On earth, we dwell in this body of our humiliation, but it will undergo a change *"in a moment, in the twinkling of an eye, at the last trump: for the trumpet shall sound, and the dead shall be raised incorruptible, and we shall be changed"* (1 Corinthians 15:52). Then we will come into our glory, and the body, made suitable to the state of glory, will be appropriately called the body of glory. We do not need to pry with curiosity into the details of the change, nor attempt to define all the differences between the two states of our bodies, for *"it doth not yet appear what we shall be"* (1 John 3:2). We may be content to leave much to be made known to us later on. Yet, though *"we see through a glass, darkly"* (1 Corinthians 13:12), we nevertheless do see something and would not shut our eyes to the little we know. We do not yet know as we are known, but we do know in part (v. 12), and that partial knowledge is precious.

The gates of glory have been ajar at times, and men have looked for a while and have seen and wondered. Three times, at least, human eyes have seen something of the body of glory. The face of Moses, when he came down from the mountain, shone so that those who gathered around him could not look at it, and he had to cover it with a veil. In that luminous face of the man who had been in high communion with God for forty days, they saw some gleams of the brightness of glorified man. Our Lord made a still clearer manifestation of the glorious body when He was transfigured in the presence of three of His disciples. When His garments became bright and glistening, whiter than any bleach could make them, and He Himself was all aglow with glory, His disciples saw and marveled. The face of Stephen is a third window, so to speak, through which we may look at the glory to be revealed, for even Christ's enemies thought Stephen's face looked like the face of an angel as they gazed upon the martyr in his confession of the Lord. These three transient gleams of the morning light may serve as symbols for us in order to help us form some faint idea of what the body of the glory of Christ is, and what the body of our own glory will be in the future.

In that marvelous Scripture passage of 1 Corinthians 15, in which the veil seems to be lifted higher than it ever has been before or since, we learn a few specifics that are worthy to be repeated. While the body is here below, it is corruptible, subject to decay. It gradually becomes weak through old age, and at last it yields to the blows of death, falls into the ground, and becomes the food of worms. But the new body will be incorruptible; it will not be subject to any process of disease, decay, or decline, and it will never, through the ages, yield to the force of death. It will be the immortal companion to the immortal spirit.

There are no graves in heaven. No funeral toll will ever sadden the New Jerusalem. On earth, the body is weak. The apostle Paul said, *"It is sown in weakness"* (1 Corinthians 15:43). It is subject to all sorts of infirmities in life, and in death it loses all strength. It is weak in performing our own will, weaker still in performing the heavenly will; it is weak in performing and weak in suffering, but it is to be *"raised in power"* (v. 43). All infirmity will be completely removed. We do not need to speculate about how much of this power will be physical and how much of it will be spiritual; we do not need to define where the material ends and the spiritual begins. We will be *"as the angels"* (Matthew 22:30), and we have found no difficulty believing that these pure spirits *"excel in strength"* (Psalm 103:20). We have had no difficulty understanding the apostle Peter when he said that angels are *"greater in power and might"* (2 Peter 2:11). Our bodies will be *"raised in power."*

173

In addition, on earth, the body is a natural or soulish body—a body fit for the soul, for the lowest faculties of our mental nature. However, according to Paul in 1 Corinthians, it is to be raised as a spiritual body, adapted to the noblest portion of our nature, suitable to be the dwelling place and the instrument of our newborn, grace-given life. This body, at present, offers no assistance to the spirit of prayer or praise; it hinders rather than helps us in spiritual disciplines. Often the spirit truly is willing, but the flesh is weak. We sleep when we ought to be attentive in prayer, and we lose heart when we should be pursuing holiness. Even the joys of the body, as well as its sorrows, tend to distract us from devotion to God. But when this body is transformed, it will be a body suitable for the highest aspirations of our perfected and glorified humanity—a spiritual body like the body of the glory of Christ.

Since the body will be sinless when it is raised, it will be without pain. Who can count how many pains we experience while we are in this house of clay? Truly, *"we that are in this tabernacle do groan"* (2 Corinthians 5:4). Does it not sometimes seem to those who are undergoing sickness as if this body were made for the purpose of suffering, as if all its nerves, tendons, veins, pulses, vessels, and valves were parts of a strange instrument upon which every note of the entire scale of pain might be played? Have patience, you who linger in this shattered dwelling, for a *"house not made with hands"* (v. 1) awaits you. In heaven there is no sorrow and sighing; the rod of discipline will no longer be used when the faultiness is altogether removed.

As the new body will be without pain, it will also withstand weariness. The body of glory will not yield to faintness or weaken through exhaustion. Is it not implied that the spiritual body does not need to sleep, when we read that the redeemed serve God *"day and night in his temple"* (Revelation 7:15)?

In a word, the bodies of believers, like the body of Christ, will be perfect. There will be nothing lacking and nothing faulty in them. If believers should die in the feebleness of age, they will not rise in the same way. Or if they should lose one of their five senses, or a limb, or become lame or maimed, they will not be this way in heaven. Regarding both body and spirit, *"they are without fault before the throne of God"* (Revelation 14:5). The statement, *"We shall be like him"* (1 John 3:2), is true of all believers, and therefore they all will be fair and beautiful and perfect. The righteous will be like Christ.

My imagination is not able to give you a picture of what it will mean to be *"changed"* (1 Corinthians 15:52) or transformed, but those who are alive and remain on earth when the Son of God returns will undergo this change, and they will enter glory without death. *"For this corruptible must put on incorruption, and this mortal must put on immortality"* (v. 53). Therefore, the bodies of living believers will pass from one state into the other in the twinkling of an eye. They will be transformed from the *"vile"* to the *"glorious,"* from the state of humiliation into the state of glory, by the power of the coming Savior.

The miracle is amazing enough when you think about it occurring to those who will be alive when Christ comes. Yet the resurrection of the dead is even more amazing. Think again about the fact that a very large number of believers will already be in their graves when the Lord appears a second time. Some of these will have been buried long enough to be decomposed. If you could remove the soil and break open the coffin lid, you would find nothing but foulness and corruption. But those decaying remains are the body of the saint's humiliation, and that very body is to be transformed into the likeness of Christ's glorious body. Admire the miracle as you examine the mighty change! Look down into the loathsome tomb, and, if you can endure it, gaze upon the decayed body. This, even this, is to be transformed into Christ's likeness. What a work this is! And what a Savior is He who will achieve it!

What marvels I see with my spiritual eyes! Indeed, it requires faith, and we thank God we have it. Again, the resurrection of Christ has forever settled in our minds, beyond all controversy, the resurrection of all who are in Him. *"For if we believe that Jesus died and rose again, even so them also which sleep in Jesus will God bring with him"* (1 Thessalonians 4:14). Still, it is a marvel of marvels, a miracle that requires the fullness of the Deity. Of whom but God, very God of very God, could it be said that He will change our bodies and make them like His glorious body?

THE POWER OF CHRIST

Secondly, let us consider the fact that the power that is to raise the dead is resident in Christ at this moment. That is what the text says: *"According to the working whereby he is able even to subdue all things unto himself."*

This is not some new power that Christ will take to Himself in the last days and then display for the first time. The power that will awaken the dead is the same power that is in Him at this moment, which is going forth from Him at this instant in the midst of His church and among the sons of men. I call this to your attention and invite you to follow the line of thought in the text.

The Power Is in Christ Now

Notice that all the power by which the last transformation will be made is even now attributed to our Lord Jesus Christ as the Savior. *"We look for the Saviour, the Lord Jesus Christ."* When Christ raises the dead, He will do so as a Savior, and it is precisely in that capacity that we need the application of His power at this moment. Settle this in your heart: we are seeking to save men, and we are not seeking a hopeless thing, for Jesus Christ, as a Savior, is able to subdue all things to Himself. The text expressly tells us so. It does not merely say that as the One who raises the dead, He is able to subdue all things, but that, as the Savior, the Lord Jesus Christ, He is able to do this. His titles are clearly given. He is presented to us as the Lord, the Savior, the Anointed; in that capacity, He is said to be able to subdue all things to Himself. This is good news for us! Beloved, in light of this, our prayers for the conversion of men may be extensive, our expectations great, and our efforts confident! Nothing is too hard for our Lord Jesus Christ; nothing in regard to the work of salvation is beyond His power. If, as a Savior, He will resurrect the dead in the future, He can quicken the spiritually dead even now.

The power of the Resurrection is going forth today. It is pulsating through the quickened portion of the congregations in our churches; it is filling each heart that beats with love for God; it is preserving the path of life in the souls of all the spiritual, so that they do not go back to their former death in sin. The power that will work the Resurrection will be wonderful, but it will be no new thing. At this very moment, it can be seen in operation everywhere in the church of God by those who have eyes to see it. In this, I join with the apostle Paul in his prayer,

> *That the God of our Lord Jesus Christ, the Father of glory, may give unto you the spirit of wisdom and revelation in the knowledge of him: the eyes of your understanding being enlightened; that ye may know what is the hope of his calling, and what the riches of the glory of his inheritance in the saints, and what is the exceeding greatness of his power to us-ward who believe, according to the working of his mighty power, which he wrought in Christ, when he raised him from the dead, and set him at his own right hand in the heavenly places, far above all principality, and power, and might, and dominion, and every name that is named, not only in this world, but also in that which is to come: and hath put all things under his feet, and gave him to be the head over all things to the church, which is his body, the fulness of him that filleth all in all.*
>
> *(Ephesians 1:17–23)*

All Opposition Will Be Overcome

Note next that the words of our text verse imply that opposition to this power may be expected but that all resistance will be overcome. The word *"subdue"* indicates that there is a force to be conquered and brought into subjection. *"He is able even to subdue all things unto himself."* This is astounding! There will be no opposition to the Resurrection. The trumpet sound will bring the dead from their graves, and no particle will disobey the summons. However, there is resistance to spiritual resurrection—resistance that only Omnipotence can conquer. In the conversion of sinners, natural depravity is an opposing force, for men have their hearts set upon their sins, and they do not love the things of God; neither will they listen and respond to the voice of mercy.

Beloved, to remove all our fears concerning our Lord's ability to save, the text says, *"he is able"*—not only able to raise all things from the dead, but also *"to subdue all things unto himself."* Here again, I ask you to take the encouragement the text presents to you. If there is opposition to the Gospel, He is able to subdue it. In one man there may be prejudice; another man's heart may be darkened with error. One man may hate the very name of Jesus; another may be so wedded to his sins that he cannot part from them. Others may be very determined in their opposition. Yet, the text meets every situation. *"He is able even to subdue all things"*—to conquer them, to break down the barriers that try to prevent the display of His power, and to make those very barriers the means of manifesting that power even more gloriously. *"He is able even to subdue all things."*

All Can Be Saved by His Power

Observe also that the language of our text includes all possible cases. *"He is able even to subdue all things unto himself"*—not one or two things here and there, but *"all things."* There is no one in this world who is so fallen, debased, depraved, and willfully wicked, that Jesus cannot save him, not even if he lives beyond the reach of ordinary ministry through the church. Jesus can bring the heathen to the Gospel, or the Gospel to them. The wheels of providence can be arranged in such a way that salvation will be brought to the outcasts; even war, famine, and plague may become messengers for Christ, for He, too, rides upon *"the wings of the wind"* (2 Samuel 22:11).

The text verse suggests a parallel between the Resurrection and the subduing of all things. The Resurrection will be accomplished by divine power, and the salvation of sinners is effected in the same way. All men are dead in sin, but He can raise them. Many of them are corrupt with immorality, but He can transform them. Some of them are, so to speak, lost to all hope; like a dead body that has been scattered to the winds, they are desperate cases for whom even pity seems to waste her sighs. But He who will raise all manner of the dead can raise sinners of all kinds by the same power, with just a word. And as the dead will become like Christ when they are raised, the wicked are made to be like Jesus when they are converted.

Brilliant examples of virtue can be found in those who used to be terrible examples of vice; the most depraved and reprobate will become the most devout and earnest. What a leap there is from the vile body to the body of glory, and what a distance there is from the sinner who is damned in lust to the saint who is bright with the radiance of sanctity! The leap seems very far, but Omnipotence can bridge the gulf. The Savior, the Lord Jesus Christ, is able to do it. He is able to do it in millions of cases, able to do it at this very moment.

A few years ago in Perugia, Italy, there lived a man who had the loosest morals and the worst conceivable disposition. He had given up all religion; he loathed God, and had arrived at such a desperate state of mind that he had developed an affection for the Devil and had determined to worship the Evil One. Imagining Satan to be the image and embodiment of all rebellion, freethinking, and lawlessness, he deified him in his own mind and desired nothing more than to be a devil himself.

On one occasion, a Protestant missionary had been preaching in Perugia. A priest happened to say in this apostate man's hearing that there were Protestants in Perugia, and therefore the city was being defiled by heretics. "And who do you think Protestants are?" the priest asked. Then, answering his own question, he said, "They are men who have renounced Christ and who worship the Devil." This was an absolute and outrageous lie, but it had far different results than its author intended. When the man heard this, he thought, "Oh, then I will go and meet with them, for I am very much in agreement with them," and away he went to the Protestant meeting, in the hope of finding an assembly that propagated lawlessness and worshipped the Devil. But there he heard the Gospel and was saved.

In this example and in ten thousand cases that are equally as remarkable, we can see the ability of our King to *"subdue all things unto himself."* How can any man whom God ordains to save, escape from eternal love that is as omnipresent as God Himself? If His sword cannot reach the ones who are far away, His arrows can, and they are sharp in His enemy's hearts even now. No boastful Goliath can stand before our David. Even though the weapon that He uses today may be only a stone from the brook, the Philistine will be subdued. There may be an agnostic, an atheist, or even a lover of the Devil, but if he is only a man, mercy can still come to him. Jesus Christ is able to subdue him unto Himself. None have gone too far, and none are too hardened. While Christ lives in heaven, we never need to despair of any who are still in this mortal life. *"He is able even to subdue all things unto himself."*

Jesus Will Do It All

You will observe that the text does not say that the means of salvation are inadequate. I am often concerned that souls might not be saved through my ministry because of deficiencies in myself. I fear that I might not be prayerful or energetic or earnest enough, or that it might be said, "[Jesus] *did not many mighty works there because of their unbelief*" (Matthew 13:58). But the text seems to obliterate man altogether. *"He is able even to subdue all things unto himself"*—that is to say, Jesus does it, Jesus can do it, Jesus will do it all.

By the weakest means, Jesus can work mightily; He can take hold of us, unfit as we are for service, and make us fit. He can grasp us in our foolishness and teach us wisdom; He can take us in our weakness and make us strong. Beloved, if we had to find resources for ourselves, and if we had to rely upon ourselves, our efforts might well be renounced. However, since He is able, we will cast the burden of this work on Him. We will go to Him in faith and prayer, asking Him to work mightily through us to the praise of His glory.

The Savior Is Able Right Now

In addition, note that the text says that Christ has the ability to subdue right now. I have already pointed this out to you, but I refer to it again. The Resurrection is a matter of the future, but the power that will accomplish the Resurrection is a matter of the present. *"According to the working whereby he is able even to subdue all things unto himself,"* Jesus is as strong now as He will ever be, for He does not change. At this moment, He is just as able to convert souls as at the time of the brightest revival, or at Pentecost itself. There are no ebbs and flows with Christ's power. Omnipotence is in the hand that was pierced, and it remains there permanently. Oh, if only we could awaken it. If only we could bring the Captain of the Host to the battlefield again—to fight for His church, to work through His servants! What marvelous things we would see, for *"he is able."* We are not hindered in Him; we are hindered in ourselves if we are hindered at all.

Let us earnestly pray to our Lord, for He only has to will it and thousands of sinners will be saved. Let us lift up our hearts to Him who only has to speak the word and whole nations will be born to Him. The resurrection of mankind will not be a work that occupies centuries; it will be accomplished immediately. The same thing may happen in our churches, throughout the nations, and throughout the world. Christ may do a quick and great work, to the amazement of all who see it. He may send the rod of His strength out of Zion and rule in the midst of His enemies (Psalm 110:2). He may unmask His artillery, discharge His mines, advance His boundaries, subdue the city of His adversaries, and ride victoriously through the Bozrah of His foes (Jeremiah 49:13). Who will hold back His hand? *"Who will say unto him, What doest thou?"* (Job 9:12).

THE WORK TO BE ACCOMPLISHED

I said that I would ask you to consider, in the third place, the work that we desire to see accomplished. Beloved, we long to see the Savior bringing souls to Himself—not bringing them to our way of thinking or to our churches or to honor our powers of persuasion, but *"unto himself."*

I now want to directly apply our text to those of you who do not yet know Christ. Oh, sinner, how I wish that you were subdued to Jesus, that you would kiss those dear feet that were nailed to the cross for you, that you would love, in life, Him who loved you even to the point of death. It would be a blessed subjection. There never was a subject of an earthly monarch who was happier in his king than you would be. As God is our witness, we who preach the Gospel do not want to subdue you to ourselves, as though we would rule you and be lords over your spirit. It is to Jesus, to Jesus only, that we want you to be subdued. If you only desired this subjection, it would be liberty and peace and joy to you!

Notice that this subjection is to be desired very highly, since it involves transformation. Understand the meaning of the text. Christ transforms the *"vile body"* into *"his glorious body,"* and this is part of subjecting all things unto Himself. But do you call this subjection? Is this not a subjection that is to be longed for with an insatiable desire: to be so subdued by Christ that I, a poor, vile sinner, may become like Him—holy, harmless, undefiled? This is the subjection that I desire for you who are unconverted. I trust that I have felt it myself, and I pray that you may feel it, too. He is able to give it to you. Ask Him for it at once. Say the prayer right now; believe that the Savior can work the transformation in you right now, at this very moment. And, my brothers and sisters in the faith, have faith for the salvation of sinners. Plead for them, so that this subjection and conquering, which will actually uplift and liberate them, may be accomplished in them.

For, remember that to be subjected to Christ is, according to our text, to be made suitable for heaven. He will change the body of our humiliation and make it like the body of His glory. The body of glory is a body appropriate for glory, a body that participates in glory. The Lord Jesus can make you, sinner, equipped for heaven and suitable for glory, even though you are now in a condition suitable for hell. He can breathe into you now an anticipation of that glory, in the joy and peace of mind that His pardon will bring to you.

It must be a very sad thing to be a soldier under any circumstances. To have to kill and subdue, even in a righteous cause, is cruel work. However, to be a soldier of King Jesus is an honor and a joy. The service of Jesus is a noble service. Beloved, I have been earnestly seeking to capture your heart for Jesus. It has been a long and weary battle. I have summoned you to surrender, and have opened fire upon you with the Gospel, but perhaps it has still been in vain. I have striven to throw a few live shells into the very heart of your city, in the form of warnings and cautions and pleading. But, oh, how I wish I could burst open the gates of your heart today, to allow Prince Immanuel to come in. He who is at your gates is not a foreign monarch; He is your rightful Prince, your Friend and Lover. It will not be a strange face that you will see when Jesus comes to reign in you. When the King in His beauty wins your soul, you will think you are a fool a thousand times over that you did not receive Him before. Instead of being afraid that He will ransack your soul, you will open all its doors and invite Him to search each room. You will exclaim, "Take everything, Blessed Monarch, for it will belong to me most when it is Yours. Take everything, and reign and rule."

I propose terms of surrender to you. They are only these: yield yourself to Christ, give up your works and ways, both good and bad, trust in Him to save you, and be His servant from this time on. While I invite you, I trust He is speaking through me to you and will win you to Himself. I am not pleading in vain; I am relying on the delightful encouragement of our text, *"He is able even to subdue all things unto himself."* May He prove His power today.

Chapter Ten

The Coming Resurrection

Marvel not at this: for the hour is coming, in the which
all that are in the graves shall hear his voice, and shall
come forth; they that have done good, unto the resurrec-
tion of life; and they that have done evil, unto the
resurrection of damnation.
—John 5:28–29

It is vital for us to keep in mind that the doctrine of the resurrection of the dead is distinctively a Christian belief. A few philosophers talked about the immortality of the spirit, assisted by their natural reason and a little light that lingered in tradition or that was borrowed from the Jews. However, the belief that the body will rise again, that there will be another life for this physical frame, is a hope that was brought to light by the revelation of Christ Jesus. Men could not have imagined something so marvelous, and they prove their powerlessness to have invented it by the fact that when they hear of it for the first time, they still resort to mocking, as they did with the apostle Paul at Athens (Acts 17:32). *"Can these* [dry] *bones live?"* (Ezekiel 37:3), is still the unbeliever's sneer.

The doctrine of the Resurrection is a lamp that has been lit by the hand that was once pierced by nails on the cross. It is linked in our holy faith with the person of Jesus Christ, and it is one of the brightest gems in His crown. Perhaps I should call it the signet ring, the seal by which He has proven conclusively that He has the King's authority and has come from God.

The doctrine of the Resurrection is vital to the Gospel, and it ought to be preached in our churches much more often than it is. Read how the apostle Paul described the Gospel that he preached, and by which true believers are saved:

> *I delivered unto you first of all that which I also received, how that Christ died for our sins according to the scriptures; and that he was buried, and that he rose again the third day according to the scriptures.*   *(1 Corinthians 15:3–4)*

From the resurrection of Christ, Paul argued that all the dead will also be raised. And he insisted that if Christ is not risen, both the faith of believers who have died and his own preaching were in vain. In the early church, the doctrine of the Resurrection was the main weapon of war that preachers used. Wherever the first missionaries went, they stated prominently that there would be a judgment and that the dead would rise again to be judged by the Man Christ Jesus, according to the Gospel. If we desire to honor Christ Jesus, the Risen One, we must give prominence to this truth.

Moreover, the doctrine is continually blessed by God to awaken the minds of men. When we think that our actions are confined to this present life, we are careless about them, but when we discover that they are far-reaching and that they cast influences for good or evil across an eternal destiny, then we regard them more seriously. What trumpet call can be more startling, what stirring voice can be more awakening, than this news to the indifferent sinner that there is life after death, that men must stand *"before the judgment seat of Christ; that every one may receive the things done in his body, according to that he hath done, whether it be good or bad"* (2 Corinthians 5:10)?

In this chapter, I will try to explain the doctrine of the resurrection of the dead for just such purposes—to honor Christ and to awaken the indifferent. I would not want you to finish this book without receiving new life in Christ, without having a sure hope of resurrection. May God give me success in this. Let me begin by explaining what our text means. Then, secondly, let me try to explain what it teaches us.

DO NOT BE SURPRISED

To begin, we will take each word of our text and weigh its meaning. Observe, then, that Jesus forbids us to be astonished. *"Marvel not at this."* Let us understand the background of our Savior's words. He had just been speaking of the two ways of giving life that belonged to Him as the Son of Man. The first was the power to raise the dead from their graves to a renewed, natural life. He proved this on several occasions in His lifetime: at the gates of Nain, when He met the funeral procession of the widow's son; in the room of the dead daughter of Jairus; and again at the tomb of the almost-decaying Lazarus. Jesus had power when He was on earth, and He still has power, if He should so will it, to speak to those who have departed and to command them to return again to this mortal state and to reassume the joys and sorrows and duties of life. *"As the Father raiseth up the dead, and quickeneth them; even so the Son quickeneth whom he will"* (John 5:21).

189

After our Lord had spoken for a moment on that part of His life-giving ability, He moved on to a second aspect of it, and He testified that the time had arrived when His voice was being heard for the quickening of the spiritually dead:

Verily, verily, I say unto you, he that heareth my word, and believeth on him that sent me, hath everlasting life, and shall not come into condemnation; but is passed from death unto life. Verily, verily, I say unto you, the hour is coming, and now is, when the dead shall hear the voice of the Son of God: and they that hear shall live.   *(John 5:24–25)*

We see in the Gospels that the spiritually dead—those who are dead to holiness and dead to faith, dead to God and dead to grace; those who lie enshrouded in the grave clothes of evil habits, rotting in the coffins of their depravity, deep down in the graves of their transgressions—are made alive when Jesus speaks. A spiritual life is given to them. Their dead spirits are raised out of their long and horrible sleep, and they are enlivened with the life of God.

Now, both of these forms of quickening are worthy to be marveled at. The resurrection of the natural man to natural life is a very amazing thing. Yet, to raise a dead spirit to spiritual life—this is more amazing, by far!

To you, dear believers in the faith, the quickening of the dead is not as astonishing as the saving of dead spirits, and, indeed, it is true that the raising up of a corpse from the grave is by no means as astounding as the raising up of a dead spirit from the sleep of sin. When a dead spirit is saved, the elements of death within the spirit are potent. They resist the life-giving power of

grace, so that regeneration is a victory as well as a creation, a complicated miracle, a glorious display of both
grace and power.

Those who are believers may humbly learn one lesson from this. By nature, we ourselves are very much
like the Jews of Jesus' day. We question mistrustfully;
we unbelievingly wonder when we see or hear of new
displays of the greatness of our Lord Jesus Christ. Our
hearts are so narrow that we cannot receive His glory in
its fullness. Yes, we love Him and we trust Him; we believe that He is the most beautiful and the greatest and
the best and the mightiest, but if we had a fuller view of
what He can do, our amazement very probably would be
mingled with a large amount of doubt.

As yet, we have only vague ideas of our Lord's glory
and power. We believe in the doctrine of His deity; we
are orthodox enough, but we have not thoroughly real-
ized the fact that He is Lord God Almighty. Does it not
sometimes seem impossible to you that certain griev-
ously ungodly people could be converted? But how can it
be impossible with Him who can raise the dead? Does it
not seem impossible that you could ever be sustained
through your present trouble? But how can it be impossible with Him who will make the dry bones live and
cause the sepulcher to give up its dead? It appears im-
probable at times that your depravity will ever be
cleansed and that you will be perfect and *"without spot"*
(1 Peter 1:19). But why? He who is able to present tens
of thousands of bodies before His throne—bodies that
have slept in the sepulcher for a long time and have decayed into dust—what can He not accomplish within His
people?

Oh, doubt no more, and do not let even the greatest
wonders of His love, His grace, His power, or His glory

cause you to be astonished and to disbelieve. Rather, say, as each new extraordinary display of His divine power rises before you, "I expected this of Him. I gathered that He could achieve this, for I understood that He is able to subdue all things to Himself. I knew that He formed the worlds and built the heavens and guided the stars, and that by Him all things hold together (Colossians 1:16–17). I am not, therefore, astounded when I see the greatest marvels of His power." The first words of the text, then, urge us to have faith, and they rebuke all amazement and unbelief.

THE HOUR IS COMING

I now call your attention to the second theme of our text. *"The hour is coming,"* said Christ. I suppose He calls it an *"hour"* in order to intimate how very near it is in His estimation, since we do not pay attention to the exact time of an event when it is extremely remote. An event that will not occur for hundreds of years is at first noted and anticipated by the year. Only when we are reasonably near to it do people talk about the day of the month in which it will occur, and we are getting very near to it when we inquire about the precise hour.

Christ declared to us that, whether we think so or not, in God's mind the day of resurrection is very near. It may be a thousand years off, even now, yet to God it is only one day (2 Peter 3:8). Christ wants us to try to think God's thoughts about it; He does not want us to consider any amount of time to be long, since time is short by its very nature and will be regarded in that way by us when it is past and the day has arrived. It is practical and wise for us to come face-to-face with what is inevitable and to act as though it were as soon as tomorrow morning that the trumpet would sound and we would be judged.

"The hour is coming," said the Savior. With these words, He taught us the certainty of that judgment. The hour is coming; it assuredly is coming. In the divine decree, this is the day for which all other days were made. Even if it were possible that any decision of the Almighty could be changed, this one never will, for the Scripture says,

> He hath appointed a day, in the which he will judge the world in righteousness by that man whom he hath ordained; whereof he hath given assurance unto all men, in that he hath raised him from the dead. *(Acts 17:31)*

"The hour is coming." Reflect on these words, beloved. That most solemn hour is coming closer every moment. Every second brings it nearer. While you have been reading these words, you have been carried toward that great event. As the pendulum of time continues to beat unceasingly, as morning dawn gives way to evening shade, and as the seasons follow in constant cycle, we are being carried along the river of time, nearer to the ocean of eternity. As if I am being carried on the wings of some mighty angel who never pauses in his matchless flight, I journey onward toward the judgment seat of God. Beloved, by that same flight, you are also being hurried on. Look to the Resurrection, then, as a thing that is constantly coming closer, that is silently drawing nearer and nearer, hour by hour. Such contemplation will be of the utmost benefit to you.

Our Lord's words read as if the one hour of which He spoke completely drives into obscurity all other events, as if the hour—the one hour, the last hour, the hour *par excellence,* the master hour, the royal hour—was of all hours the only hour that was worth mentioning as being inevitable and important. Like Aaron's rod, the judgment hour swallows up every other hour (Exodus 7:10–12). We hear of hours that have been momentous in determining the fate of nations, hours in which the welfare of millions trembled in the balance, hours in which the die had to be cast for peace or war, hours that have been called crises in history, and we are apt to think that periods such as this occur frequently in the history of the world. Yet, here is the culminating crisis of all, here is the iron hour of severity, the golden hour of truth, the clear sapphire hour of disclosure.

In that majestic hour, the impartial decisions of the Lord Jesus Christ with regard to all the spirits and bodies of men will be proclaimed. Oh, what an extraordinary hour is quickly advancing! My dear brothers and sisters, every now and then I earnestly wish that I could be eloquent. I wish this right now so that I might, on such a theme as this, fire your imaginations and inflame your hearts. However, let me urge you to assist me now for a moment. Since this hour is coming, try to think of it as very, very near. Suppose it were to come right now; suppose that even now the dead were to rise, that in an instant you and I will be melted into an infinitely great gathering of peoples, and that all eyes will be focused upon the great descending Judge, sitting in majesty upon His Great White Throne. I implore you to think of yourself in this context: the curtain of eternity is being raised at this moment. Anticipate the sentence that will come forth to you from the throne of righteousness; imagine that at this precise moment it were being pronounced upon you! And now, I urge you to examine yourself, just as though times of testing had come, for such an examination will be to your soul's benefit if you are saved, and it may awaken your spirit if you are unconverted.

The Coming Resurrection

ALL WILL RISE

Thirdly, what did Jesus mean when He said, *"All that are in the graves shall hear his voice"*? *"All"* does not only mean all whose bodies are actually in the grave at this time, but all who ever have been buried, even though they may have been uprooted from their graves and their bones may have mingled with the elements, been scattered by the winds, dissolved in the waves, or absorbed into the vegetation. All who have lived and died will certainly rise again. All! Try to compute the numberless number! Try to count the countless! How many people lived before the Flood? It has been believed, and I think accurately, that the inhabitants of this world were more numerous at the time of the Flood than they are now, due to the enormous length of human life in those days. The number of men was not so terribly thinned out by death as it is now.

Think, if you will, from the time of the Flood onward, of all of Adam's descendants. From Tarshish to Egypt, men covered the lands. Nineveh, Babylon, Chaldea, Persia, Greece, Rome—these were vast empires of men. Who can count the multitudes of Parthians, Scythians, and Tartars who lived? As for those northern swarms of Goths and Huns and Vandals, in the Middle Ages they were continually streaming as from a teeming hive. The Franks and Saxons and Celts also multiplied in turn. Yet, these nations were only types of a numerous group of nations that were even more populous. Think of Ethiopia and the whole continent of Africa; remember India and Japan. In all lands, great tribes of men have come and have gone to rest in their sepulchers. What millions upon millions must lie buried in China and Burma! What innumerable multitudes are slumbering in the land of the pyramids, in the tombs of the mummies! Who can compute the number of everyone, both great and small, who was embalmed from ancient times in Egypt?

Hear, then, and believe; out of all who have ever lived, not one will be left in the tomb. All—yes, all—will rise. I may well say, as the psalmist did of another matter, *"Such knowledge is too wonderful for me; it is high, I cannot attain unto it"* (Psalm 139:6). How has God marked all of these bodies; how has He tracked the remains of each one? How will Jesus Christ be able to raise all of them? I do not know, but He will do it, for He declared it and God has purposed it. *"All that are in the graves shall hear his voice."* All the righteous, all the wicked; all who were engulfed in the sea, all who slumber on the lap of the earth; all the powerful ones, all the multitudes of servants and slaves; all the wise and all the foolish; all the beloved and all the despised—there will not be one single individual omitted.

My dear friend, it may be best for you to look at the question in a more personal light. You will not be forgotten; your separated spirit will have its appointed place, and the body that once contained it will be guarded until, by the power of God, it will be restored to your spirit again when the last trumpet sounds. You, my friend, will rise again. As surely as you are alive right now, you will stand before the once-crucified Son of Man. It is not possible that you will be forgotten; you will not be permitted to rot away into annihilation, to be left in the darkness of obscurity. We must, we will, rise, each and every one of us, without a single exception. This is an amazing truth, and yet we should not be amazed at it in the sense that we doubt it, though we may be in awe of it and admire the Lord who will bring it to pass.

"All that are in the graves shall hear his voice."
Hear? How can this be? A thousand years ago, a man was
buried, and not the slightest trace of his ears remains—
all has vanished. Will those ears ever hear? Yes, for He
who caused them to hear in the first place worked just as
amazing a thing when He created them as He will when
He makes them hear for a second time. It took God to
make the hearing ears of the newborn baby; it will require nothing less than God to renew the hearing ears
the second time. Yes, the ears that were lost in silence
for so long will hear! And what will be the sound that
will startle those newly awakened and freshly fashioned
ears? It will be the voice of the Son of God, the voice of
Jesus Christ Himself.

This passage of Scripture teaches us of the dullness
of human nature and how depraved the heart is. It also
reminds those who are careless that there is no escape
for them. If you will not hear the voice of Jesus now, you
will have to hear it then. You may plug up your ears today, but there will be no doing that in the Day of the last
trumpet; on that Day, you will have to hear. Oh, if only
you would hear now! You are going to hear the summons
to judgment. Yet, I pray that you may instead hear the
summons to mercy and become obedient to it and live.
"All that are in the graves shall hear his voice." Notice
that it says *"shall hear,"* and not *"might hear."* No matter who a person may have been, he will become subject
to the power of God's omnipotent command and will appear before His sovereign judgment seat.

ALL WILL COME FORTH

Note the next words, *"And shall come forth."* This
means, of course, that their bodies will come out of the

grave: out of the earth or the water or the air or wherever else their bodies may be. But I think that even more than that is intended by the words, *"shall come forth."* The phrase seems to imply a manifestation, as though the deceased have been here all the time and were only hidden and concealed in their graves. However, as *"the voice of the LORD maketh the hinds to calve, and discovereth the forests"* (Psalm 29:9), the voice of God in resurrection will reveal the secrets of men and will cause them to bring forth their truest selves into the light, to be revealed to all. The hypocrite, masked villain that he is, is not revealed now, but when the voice of Christ sounds, he will come forth in a sense that will be horrible to him. He will be deprived of all the embellishments of his masquerade; the mask of his false profession of faith will be torn away. He will stand before men and angels as if he had leprosy on his face—an object of universal derision, abhorred by God and despised by men.

Dear reader, are you ready to come forth right now? Would you be willing to have your heart revealed? Would you wear it on your sleeve for all to see? Is there not much about you that could not bear the light of the sun? How much more will those things not be able to bear the light of Him whose eyes are as a flame of fire (Revelation 1:14), seeing all and testing all by a close examination in which He cannot be mistaken! Your coming forth on that Day will not only be a reappearance from the shadows of the sepulcher, but also a coming forth into the light of heaven's truth, which will reveal you with the brightness of midday.

ALL WILL RETAIN THEIR FORMER CHARACTER

The text goes on to say that all who will come forth will be in one of two categories: those who have done good and those who have done evil. From this, we must understand the next truth, that death does not change a person's character and that after death we must not expect improvements to occur. Those who were holy will still be holy, and those who were filthy will still be filthy. If they were people who had done good when they were put into the grave, they will rise as people who have done good; if they were those who had done evil when they were buried, they will rise as those who have done evil. Therefore, do not expect any room for repentance after this life; there will be no opportunities for reformation, no further proclamations of mercy or doors of hope. It is now or never with you. Remember that.

In addition, note that only two types of people will rise, for indeed there are only two types of people who ever lived, and therefore there are only two types of people who are buried and two who will rise again: those who have done good and those who have done evil. Why is there no mention of anyone of mixed character, whose conduct was neither good nor evil, or was both good and evil? It is because no one like this exists. You may ask, "Good people sometimes do evil, do they not? May not some who are evil still do good?" My answer to the first question is this: he who does good is a man who, having believed in Jesus Christ and received the new life, does good in his new nature and with his newborn spirit, with all the intensity of his heart. As for his sins and infirmities, into which he falls because of his old nature, these have been washed away by the precious blood of Jesus and will not be mentioned in the Day of Judgment. He will rise up as a man who has done good; his good will be remembered, but the evil will be washed away.

As for the question about those who are evil but still do good, this is my reply: they may do good in the judgment of their fellowmen, and they may do good toward their fellow mortals, but those who have evil hearts cannot do good toward God. If the fountain is defiled, every stream is necessarily polluted also. *Good* is a word that may be measured according to those who use it. The evil man's good is good toward you, his child, his wife, his friend; yet, he still has no regard for God, no reverence, no esteem for the great Lawgiver. Therefore, what may be good to you may be evil to God, because it hasn't been done for the right motive; it may even have been done with the wrong motive so that the man is dishonoring God while he is helping his friend. God will judge men by their works, but there will be only two types of people—the good and the evil. For this reason, each person is called to the solemn task of knowing what the general tenor of his life has been, what the true verdict regarding his *entire* life is. He must know where he is heading in regard to eternity, and he must wholeheartedly turn to Christ if he has not yet yielded to Him.

Some of you reading this have many excellent qualities and virtues; however, you have never done good as God measures good, for you have never regarded God and honored Him; you have never even confessed that you have dishonored Him. In fact, you have remained proudly indifferent to God's judgment of you as a sinner, and you have set yourself up as being all that you should be. How can it be possible, while you disbelieve your God, for you to do anything that pleases Him? Your whole life is evil in God's sight—only evil. And as for you who fear His name, or who believe you do, I implore you to seriously consider your actions, since there are only two kinds of people: those who have done good and those who have done evil. Make it clear to your conscience, make it clear to the judgment of those who observe the way in which you live your life (though this is of less importance), and make it clear before God that your works are good, that your heart is right, because your outward conduct is conformed to the law of God.

ALL WILL BE JUDGED BY THEIR WORKS

Note also that the method of judgment is remarkable. Those who search the Scriptures know that the judgment at the Last Day will be entirely according to works. Will men then be saved for their works? No, by no means. Salvation is in every case the work and gift of grace. But the judgment will be guided by our works. It is right and just that all those who will be judged should be tried by the same rule. Now, no rule can be common to saints and sinners except the rule of their moral conduct, and by this rule all men will be judged. My friend, if God does not find any holiness of life in you whatsoever, He will not accept you. Someone may say, "What about the thief who was crucified with Jesus?" The righteousness of faith was in him, and it produced all the holy acts that the circumstances allowed. At the very moment in which he believed in Christ, he professed Christ and spoke for Christ, and those acts were established as evidence that he was a friend of God, while all his sins were washed away. May God grant you grace to confess your sins and to believe in Jesus, so that you may be forgiven of all your transgressions.

There must be some evidence of your faith at the Judgment. Before the multitudes of men who will be assembled at the throne of God, no evidence of your faith will be drawn from your inward feelings; rather, the evidence will be found in your outward actions. It will still be,

For I was an hungered, and ye gave me meat: I was thirsty, and ye gave me drink: I was a stranger, and ye took me in: naked, and ye clothed me: I was sick, and ye visited me: I was in prison, and ye came unto me. *(Matthew 25:35–36)*

Give careful attention, then, to practical godliness, and abhor all preaching that treats holiness of life as a secondary thing. We are justified by faith, but not by a dead faith. The faith that justifies is that which produces holiness, for *"without* [holiness] *no man shall see the Lord"* (Hebrews 12:14). Therefore, take note of the two classes into which men will be divided, and of the stern standard by which God will judge them. Then judge yourself so that you will not be condemned with the wicked.

ALL WILL RECEIVE A RESURRECTION

Finally, the different destinies of the two kinds of people are also mentioned in the text. The good will rise to *"the resurrection of life."* This does not mean mere existence, for both the good and the evil will exist, and exist forever. However, when properly understood, the word *"life"* in this Scripture passage means happiness, power, activity, privilege, capacity. In fact, it is a term so comprehensive that I would need many pages to express all that it means. There is a death in life that the ungodly will have, but the redeemed will have a life in life. It will be a true life. It will not be merely an existence, but an existence in energy, in honor, in peace, in blessedness, in perfection. This is the *"resurrection of life."*

As for the ungodly, there is a resurrection to damnation in which their bodies and souls will come clearly under the condemnation of God. To use our Savior's word, they will be damned. Oh, what a dreadful resurrection! Yet, we cannot escape from it *"if we neglect so great salvation"* (Hebrews 2:3). What a blessing it would be for an ungodly man if, when he died, he could lie down and sleep and never wake up again. Oh, if that grave could be the last of him and, like a dog, he might never awaken, what a blessing he would receive! But it is a blessing that is not yours, and never can be. Your soul must live, and your body must live. I urge you to *"fear him which is able to destroy both soul and body in hell"* (Matthew 10:28). *"Yea, I say unto you, Fear him"* (Luke 12:5).

VITAL TRUTHS FROM THE TEXT

I want to conclude by focusing on some vital lessons from our text. First, our Lord deserves our adoration and reverence. If it is true that all the dead will rise at the voice of Christ, let us worship Him. What a Savior is He who bled upon the cross! How gloriously exalted is He who was despised and rejected! Oh, beloved, if we could even lift ourselves up enough to see the hem of this truth—that He will raise all the dead out of their graves—if we would only begin to perceive the magnificence of what this means, I think we would fall at the Savior's feet, as John did when he said, *"I fell at his feet as dead"* (Revelation 1:17). Oh, what amazing power is Yours, my Lord and Master. What great honor is due to You. All glory to you, Immanuel! You have the keys of death and of hell. My soul loves and adores You. You are the ever great enthroned Prince, the Wonderful, the Counselor, the King of Kings and Lord of Lords.

Next, we are reminded again that there is comfort for our wounded hearts concerning our departed friends. We never mourn regarding the spirits of the righteous, for they are forever with the Lord. The only mourning that we permit among Christians concerns the body, which shrivels like a withered flower. When we read that famous fifteenth chapter of 1 Corinthians at funerals, we do not find it comforting with regard to the immortal spirit, for we do not need comfort about that, but we find much comfort in it with regard to the body: what is *"sown in dishonour"* will be *"raised in glory"* (1 Corinthians 15:43).

Your loved ones who have died will live; that decaying dust will live again. Do not weep as though you had cast your treasure into the sea, where you could never find it. In effect, you have only stored it in a casket, from which you will receive it again brighter than before. You will look again with your own eyes into those eyes that have spoken love to you so often, but that are now closed in the darkness of death. Your child will see you again. You will recognize your child; the same body will rise. Your departed friend will come back to you, and since he has loved his Lord as you do, you will rejoice with him in the land where there is no more death. It is only a short parting, but it will be an eternal meeting. We will be forever with the Lord, and we will also be forever with each other. Let us comfort one another, then, with these words.

Lastly, there is the lesson of self-examination. If we are to rise, some to rewards and some to punishments, then what will be your destiny? Let your conscience ask you this question: "Where will I be in eternity?" How do you feel, my friend, about the prospect of rising again? Does the thought give you any spark of joy, or does it create a measure of alarm? If your heart trembles at the thought, how will you bear it when the real fact is before you, and not merely the thought? How have you lived your life? If you will be judged by your life, of what has it consisted? What has been its guiding principle up until now? Have you believed God? Do you live by faith in the Son of God? I know you are imperfect, but are you earnestly seeking to live a holy life? Do you desire to honor God? The answer to the following question will determine how your life will be judged: what was the purpose and aim and inclination and goal of your life? Yes, there has been imperfection, but has there been sincerity? Has grace, divine grace that washes sinners in the blood of Christ, proven itself to be in you by alienating you from the sins you used to love and by leading you to love and serve God in ways that you once neglected?

I will ask you another question. If you do not feel happy at the thought of your own resurrection, are you quite peaceful concerning the resurrection of all others? Are you prepared to meet before God those with whom you have sinned during your life on earth? Here is a thought worthy of the sinner's consideration: how terrifying it will be for men and women to have to meet the companions of their sins! Was this not the real reason that the rich man wanted Lazarus to be sent back to the world to warn his five brothers so that they would not come into the place of torment? (See Luke 16:19–31.) Was he not afraid to see them there because their recriminations would increase his misery?

It will be a horrible thing for a man who has been an immoral villain to rise again and confront his victims whom his lusts dragged down to hell! How he will cringe as he hears them lay their damnation at his door and curse him for his lewdness! Oh, sinner, your sin is not dead and buried, and the fellow sinner with whom you joined hands in iniquity will rise to witness against you. The crime, the guilt, the punishment, and the guilty one will alike live again, and you will live forever in remorse, ruing the day in which you transgressed.

Let me ask you another question. If it will be terrible for many to see the dead rise again, how will they bear seeing Him, the Judge Himself, the Savior? Of all the men who ever lived, He is the one whom you must be the most afraid of, because it is He whom you should love the most today but whom you forget. How many times has someone pleaded with you to yield yourself to Jesus Christ, and how frequently have you given Him a flat denial? It may be that you have not quite done that, but you have postponed your decision and said, "I'll make a decision for Christ at a more convenient time." When Christ comes, how will you answer Him? Think about it. How will you answer Him? How will you excuse yourself? You would not have Him as a Savior, but you must have Him as your Judge, to pronounce your sentence. You despised His grace, but you cannot escape His wrath. If you would just look to Jesus now, you would find salvation in His glance; however, in refusing to do so, you heap up wrath for yourself, which will be poured out when He gives you that terrible but inevitable glance, of which the prophet said, *"All kindreds of the earth shall wail because of him"* (Revelation 1:7).

Oh, do not spurn Him! Do not despise the Crucified One! I pray that you will not trample upon His blood, but that you will come to Him so that, when you see Him on His throne, you may not be afraid.

Beloved, I will ask you two final questions. One of the best ways by which to learn what our future inheritance will be is to inquire what we have in the present. Do you have life now—I mean spiritual life—the life that grieves over sin, the life that trusts a Savior? If so, you will certainly have the resurrection of life. On the o hand, are you under condemnation now? For, *"he that believeth not is condemned already"* (John 3:18). Are you an unbeliever? Then you are condemned now; you will suffer *"the resurrection of damnation."* How can it be otherwise? Seek Christ, then, so that you may possess the life of God now by faith; if you do, you will enjoy that life forever. Escape condemnation now, and you will escape damnation for eternity.

God bless you with the abundance of His salvation, for Christ's sake.